TEN MASTERS OF THE SIKHS

From the beginning of creation itself, one rule of the creator has been going on. Whenever torture and injustice in this world have reached their ultimate level, some super human beings have been born, who, wit their voice and their works, have lit such a lamp of truth, whose light removes the dreadful and dense darkness of torture, injustice and sin and have guided the sad, unhappy and suffering people and compelled the torturers, tormentors, unjust and irreligious people to walk on the path of truth, religion, justice and kindness.

There is not second example of this kind of extraordinary sacrifice than those the ten leaders of the Sikhs made for the publicity and spread of their religion. Presented here, is the life sketch of the ten Sikh Gurus, who are worthy of being followed.

Diamond Pocket Books Presents
Religion, Spirituality & Sai Literature

Title	Author	Price
Mahabharata	Dr. B. R. Kishore	60.00
Ramayana	Dr. B. R. Kishore	60.00
Rigveda	Dr. B. R. Kishore	60.00
Samveda	Dr. B. R. Kishore	60.00
Yajurveda	Dr. B. R. Kishore	60.00
Atharvveda	Dr. B. R. Kishore	60.00
Hinduism	Dr. B. R. Kishore	95.00
Hindu Traditions & Beliefs (A Scientific Validity)	Dr. Bhojraj Dwivedi	150.00
Hindu Mythology and Religion (Quiz Book)	Ed. Sachin Singhal	95.00
Gods & Goddesses of India	B. K. Chaturvedi	60.00
Supreme Mother Durga (Durga Chalisa) Roman	B. K. Chaturvedi	95.00
The Hymns & Orisons of Lord Shiva (Roman)	B. K. Chaturvedi	25.00
Sri Hanuman Chalisa (Roman)	B. K. Chaturvedi	30.00
Pilgrimage Centres of India	B. K. Chaturvedi	95.00
Fast & Festivals of India	Manish Verma	50.00
Chalisa Sangrah (Roman)	R. P. Hingorani	25.00
Srimad Bhagwath Geeta (Sanskrit & English)	Dayanand Verma	50.00
Sri-Ram-Charit Manas	Ed. S. P. Ojha	120.00
Realm of Sadhana (What Saints & Masters Say)	Chakor Ajaonkar	30.00
The Spiritual Philosophy of Shri Shirdi Sai Baba Shirdi	B. Umamashwara Rao	150.00
The Immortal Fakir of Shirdi	S. P. Ruhela (Com. & Ed.)	150.00
Sai Grace and Recents Predictions	Dr. S. P. Ruhela	80.00
The Divine Glory of Shri Shirdi Sai Baba	Dr. S. P. Ruhela	150.00
Shirdi Sai : The Supreme	Dr. S. P. Ruhela	80.00
Divine Grace of Sri Shirdi Sai Baba	Dr. S. P. Ruhela	150.00
Divine Revelations of a Sai Devotee	Dr. S. P. Ruhela	50.00
The Divine Glory of Sri Shirdi Sai Baba	Chakor Ajgaonkar	40.00
Communication from the spirit of Shri Shirdi Sai Baba	Dr. S. P. Ruhela	40.00
The Footprints of Shirdi Sai	Chakor Ajgaonkar	100.00
Tales from Sai Baba's Life	Chakor Ajgaonkar	60.00
Sri Shirdi Sai Baba	B. Umamaheswara Rao	60.00
Thus Spake Sri Shirdi Sai Baba	U. Umamaheswara Rao	40.00
Sai Baba of Shirdi	B. K. Chaturvedi	60.00
Sri Sathya Sai Baba : A Biography	B. K. Chaturvedi	25.00
The Eternal Sai	B. Maaney	40.00
Sri Shirdi Sai Bhjanavali (In Roman)	Dr. S. P. Ruhela	30.00
Worship of Sri Sathya Sai Baba (In Roman)	Dr. S. P. Ruhela	90.00
His Mystery and Experiencing His Love	Dr. S. P. Ruhela	60.00
World Peace and Sri Sathya Sai Avtar	Dr. S. P. Ruhela	60.00
How to Receive Sri Sathya Sai Baba's Grace	Dr. S. P. Ruhela	100.00
The Miracle Man : Sri Sathya Sai Baba	B. K. Chaturvedi	60.00
Sri Sathya Sai Baba : Understanding Rishi Ram Ram	Yogi M. K. Spencer	100.00
Oneness with God	Yogi M. K. Spencer	90.00
Quiet Talks with the Master	Eva Bell Barber	60.00
Adventures with Evil Spirits	Joseph J. Ghosh	80.00
A Child from the Spirit world Speaks	K. H. Nagrani	10.00
Future is in Our Hand	A. Somasundaram	90.00
Fragrant Spiritual Memories of A karma Yogi	Dr. S. P. Ruhela	100.00

TEN MASTERS

Prof. Gurpreet Singh

DIAMOND POCKET BOOKS

© **Publisher**

Publisher	:	**Diamond Pocket Books Pvt. Ltd.**
		X-30, Okhla Industrial Area,
		Phase-II, New Delhi-110020.
Phone	:	011-6841033, 6822803, 6822804
Fax	:	011-6925020
E-mail	:	mverma@nde.vsnl.net.in
Website	:	www.diamondpocketbooks.com
Edition	:	2001
Price	:	Rs. 60/-
Price US $	:	4/-
Laser Typesetting	:	S.R. Computers, EPT-89, Sarojini Nagar, New De
Printed at	:	Adarsh Printers, Shahdara, Delhi-110032

-: Contents :-

1. Guru Nanak Dev Ji — 7
2. Guru Angad Dev Ji — 31
3. Guru Amar Das Ji — 41
4. Guru Ram Das Ji — 47
5. Guru Arjun Dev Ji — 51
6. Guru Hargovind Ji — 54
7. Guru Hari Rai Ji — 64
8. Gur Hari Krishna Ji — 68
9. Guru Tegh Bahadur Ji — 73
10. Guru Govind Singh Ji — 83

PUBLISHER'S NOTE

India is the land of Great Saints. Masters, Gurus and Philosophers, who had given this word a totaly new vision about the immortal value and massage of humanity. And we are adding a drop to this ocean by publishing their views and teachings in easily understandable language for the well being of our society. These great souls had departed for their heavenly abode, but they will remain in this mortal world with their teachings. Ten masters is a brief presentation of 'Ten Sikh Mastes' which is an addition to our series of literature concerned with many of these holy souls. It is our sincere dedication towards our society by giving the examples of these gems of Human Race to build not only their span of life, but to enlighten the others too.

GURU NANAK DEV JI

From the beginning of creation itself, one rule of the creator has been going on. Whenever torture and injustice in this world have reached their ultimate level, some super human beings have been born, who, wit their voice and their works, have lit such a lamp of truth, whose light removes the dreadful and dense darkness of torture, injustice and sin and have guided the sad, unhappy and suffering people and compelled the torturers, tormentors, unjust and irreligious people to walk on the path of truth, religion, justice and kindness.

There is not second example of this kind of extraordinary sacrifice than those the ten leaders of the Sikhs made for the publicity and spread of their religion. Presented here, is the life sketch of the ten Sikh Gurus, who are worthy of being followed. Lord Krishna has himself said in the Gita,

"Yadaa Yadaa hi Dharamsya, Glanirbhavati Bharata,
Abhyukthanamadharmasya, Tadaatmaanam Srijamyaham
Paritranaya Sadhunam, Vinashaya cha Dushkritam;
Dharma Sansthapanarthaya Sambhavami Yuge Yuge"

i.e. Whenever righteousness is on the decline, and unrighteousness is in the ascendant, then I body Myself forth.

In the 15th century also, India had the same condition, which had after the Mahabharata. The country had got totally devastated by the continuous attacks of the Muslims. The whole country, especially Northern India was caught up in the bonds of slavery of the Muslims. On all four sides, storms of the Muslims rulers' injustice were blowing. Hindus were being forcibly converted into Islam. In fact, not just the Hindu religion, the whole of humanity was standing on the threshold of devastation.

In that age of darkness, on the full moon night in the month of Kartik, 1469 A.D., when the shinning moon in the sky was spreading its rays and was trying to remove the darkness all around, in order to fight the darkness of atrocity, injustice and wrong, a small child was born to Kalurai Bedi's wife, Tripta Devi, in the small town of Talwandi in Punjab. After growing up, he dedicated his entire life for the destruction of atrocities and immorality being carried on in the name of fanaticism and religion.

Kalurai Bedi was the chief officer maintaining land records under Rai Dular - the ruler of Talwandi. He was extremely trust worthy. There was no shortage of wealth and property. Hence, the child's birth was celebrated with a lot of pomp and show. Tripta Devi had given birth to a baby boy many years after the birth of Nanki, her daughter. The sister used to spend a lot of time at her maternal grandfather's house. Hence, she had named her Nanki. So, the people started calling him Nanak.

Right from his childhood only, his specialities showed clearly. When his other friends used to be busy playing, the child Nanak used to sit down under a tree, close his eyes and start chanting the name of "Sat Kartar". And if a child would come and sit near him, he would include him in his chants.

At the age of five, his father made arrangements for his education. He started going to Pandit Gopal. He was so intelligent that in a few days he compelled Pandit Gopal into accepting that the child was much more knowledgeable and wise than the education that he himself had and received.

When Gopal Pandit told Mehta Kalurai about the completion of his son's education, he sent him to Maulvi Qutubuddin to study Persian. The Maulvi, too, in a few days, announced that Nanak was a wizard in the Persian language.

Pandit Gopal and Qutubuddin were both astonished to see the knowledge capability of the child Nanak. The moment Gopal Pundit asked the child Nanak to say "Om!" Nanak asked, "Pandit ji, what is the meaning of Om?" Pandit Gopal gaped at him in astonishment. He saw the Pundit troubled and said, "Shall I tell you Panditji?" "Yes." With the use of one word, Nanak explained the meaning of Om, in detail. At this, Pundit Gopal said, "You are great Nanak. Not you, but I am your pupil now." He bowed down before the wisdom of the child Nanak. It was the same with Maulvi Qutubuddin. When he started teaching Nanak, he said, "Son, read 'Alif'", he asked, "Maulvi Saheb, what is the meaning of Alif?" poor Maulvi Qutubuddin himself did not know what 'Alif' meant. In one word, Nanak explained the meaning of 'Alif'. The Maulvi went to his father and said, "Mehta, your son is himself a form of God. He can teach the whole world."

The child Nanak's knowledge and wisdom had, since his childhood, started amazing great wise men. From the beginning of life itself, such incidents had started taking place because of which people had started considering him to be a miraculous child. The belief had started settling down in people's minds that God had himself taken birth in the form of Nanak.

The 'Yagyopaveeta' (thread ceremony) is an extremely important rite amongst the Hindus, especially in the higher caste. It is considered as the second birth of a boy.

Mehta Bedi made preparations for his son's thread ceremony. However, when Gopal Pundit came to put the thread around his neck, he said, "Punditji, I do not believe in these pieces of thread. How can a few pieces of thread purify one's heart? The heart becomes pure with behaviour."

Everyone standing around was astonished to hear this. From his childhood only, Nanak was opposed to the bad practices in the name of religion that had spread in the contemporaneous Hindu society. The Brahmins had started performing many ceremonies - from birth to death - in order to earn their livelihood. Those who were rich used to fulfil these ceremonies somehow or the other. But the majority of the people could not tolerate these atrocities, committed in the name of religion. Nanak had started raising his voice against these malpractices.

Along with these religious malpractices, he, from his childhood only, had started opposing religious fanaticism and discrimination. A living example of this was Bhai Mardana, his childhood friend, who had taken birth in a Muslim family. But, without any feelings of differences, he lived throughout his life with Nanak. Wherever he went, within the country and abroad, Mardana was with him. He played a very important role in preaching and propagating the teachings and thoughts of Guru Nanak Dev. Bhai Mardana had sung the words of Nanak Dev on his 'rabab' and found a place in the hearts of the common man.

From his childhood only, Nanak's way of thinking and feelings were different from those of the other children. He would remain quiet all the time, as if deep in thought. His father saw this indifference and gave him the job of taking the animals for grazing. At dawn only, he would take the animals and go to the forest. He'd be there the whole day and return home in the evening.

It is surprising that two more great persons, before Guru Nanak Dev, had done the task of taking the animals for grazing - the ascetic Krishna and Hazrat Isa Hasih. Krishna had taken the cows for grazing in his childhood and Isa had taken the goats. Similar to them, Nanak Dev used to take buffaloes for grazing.

Nanak Dev used to take the buffaloes into the jungles and leave them there to graze. He himself used to sit down under a tree and get drowned in the thoughts of 'Sat Kartar'. One day he was sitting under a tree, deep in thought. Suddenly, he fell asleep. So, he lay down under the tree with his legs spread out and fell into a deep slumber.

Just then, Rai Dular, the ruler of Talwandi came that way on horseback. He saw a young boy sleeping under a tree and a dreadful cobra was sitting beside his head, with its fangs spread out, trying to keep the hot and sharp rays of the sun from falling on his face. Whichever way the shade of the tree would move, the cobra would spread its fangs the other way.

Rai Dular was amazed to see this scene. He understood that this young boy, lying on the grass, was no ordinary boy. When he grows up, he would either be a very big ruler, or a very big saint.

When the boy awoke, the cobra removed its hood from on top of the boy's face and quietly slithered away, into a nearby bush. On going close, Rai Dular realised that the boy was none other than the son of his chief land records maintaining officer, Mehta Kalu. From that day itself, respect and belief for Nanak sprouted in his heart.

Anyone who heard of this incident from Rai Dular was amazed. All the citizens started believing that undoubtedly, this boy was magical.

One day, Nanak took his animals for grazing. Like everyday, he left his animals and himself, went and sat down under a tree and went into meditation. There was a farmer's field closeby. The harvest was ripe. The animals saw the harvest and entered into his field to graze. They ate to their fill and trampled all the other plants. Then, they all sat down there only and started chewing their cud.

Suddenly, the owner of the field came that way. He saw that the animals had eaten the entire harvest, had trampled all the other plants and were sitting over their, chewing their cud. He caught hold of the boy Nanak, sitting in meditation under the tree and took him to Rai Dular.

"What is the matter? Why have you tied Nanak and brought him here?" Rai Dular asked.

"My Lord, his animals have ruined my entire harvest. Now, not a single grain will grow on it. I must be given compensation for this, by his father," the farmer said.

Rai Dular asked Mehta Kalu, sitting close by, to pay the loss to the farmer. Rai Dular sent his men to get an approximate idea of the loss. When these men and the farmer went to the field, the farmer was greatly surprised. Not even one plant was destroyed. The entire field was full of flourishing corp. The farmer was scared of Rai Dular's unhappiness and ran home. When the men returned and told Rai Dular that not even a single plant had been damaged, everyone was amazed. The respect that was there for Nanak Dev in Rai Dular's heart, increased even further.

After that day, Mehta Kalurai stopped sending his son to the jungle to graze the animals. Nanak Dev started living at home only, but as if he was not living in it. He would be immersed in his own thoughts.

Seeing his son so depressed, Mehta Kalurai gave him Rs.Twenty, called his childhood friend Bala and said, "Son, you go with Bala to the city and do some business there. But, whatever business you do, it must be truthful and honest. You will slowly learn how to do business."

As per his father's orders, Nanak moved towards the city with Bala. When the came near the city, they saw many saints in the forest. Nanak paid his obeisance. The sages and saints told Nanak that they were hungry. He took pity on them. He remembered his father's words and thought, "What could be better business than quenching the thirst and hunger of hungry people like these sages?" And then he gave assurance to them and went to the city with Bala to bring food for the hungry sages. When they finished eating, Nanak realised that all the money that his father had given him for business, had been spent. He said, "No business can be done without any money." And so, Bala and he decided to return to the village.

His father was astonished to see Nanak return so soon. When he asked why, his son said, "Father, you only said that whatever business you do, must be honest and truthful. According to me, no business is more honest and truthful than feeding hungry people. I finished all the money in feeding them. That is why I have come back home."

Mehta Kalurai was very angry and slapped Nanak. When Rai Dular came to know about it, he called Mehta Kalurai and expressed his unhappiness. He gave him twenty rupees and said,

"From today, Nanak is mine. Whatever loses he incurs you take them from me. But, don't say anything to Nanak. Saying this, Rai Dular's throat got choked and tears started falling from his eyes.

Mehta Kalu had only two children - son Nanak and daughter Nanki, who was many years older and was married. Her husband Jayaram used to work at a high post in Sultanpur Nawab Lodi's palace. Sultanpur was a beautiful town, set up on the banks of the River Bei, near Kapurthala. When Mehta Kalurai saw his son's sorrow, he sent him to his daughter Nanki in Sultanpur. Nanki loved her younger brother very much. She also knew that her brother was no ordinary human being. Father Kalu Mehta thought that staying with his sister, who loved him so much, Nanak's sorrow would be over. That with a change in the environment, his nature too, would change. He will start taking interest in worldly affairs and would be interested in some occupation too.

Nanki's husband was a very gentle and honest man. Hence, Nawab Lodi used to respect him a lot. After Nanak had spent some time in Sultanpur, Jayaram, after consultations with Nanki, got him a job at the palace of the Nawab. The Nawab appointed him in charge of the palace grocery and stores. Nanak would come and sit at the grocery every morning and would work till late in the night. His sister Nanki and brother-in-law Jayaram were very happy to see this and to note that he had started taking an interest in the work.

Nanak's fame, as one who helps the hungry, unclad people, had reached Sultanpur. Whenever anyone needed anything, they would go to Nanak in the stores. Nanak would help them. Hence, he had become very popular.

Seeing his growing popularity, the other employees of the Nawab were very jealous. Nawab Lodi himself was his fan. Nanak used to say, "There is no Hindu and no Turk. All the humans and animals of this world are the sons of that timeless man, who has created the world"

At that time, many provinces of India were under the occupation of the Muslims. They considered their religion superior to any other religion of the world. The fanatic Muslims were very unhappy with Nanak Dev's secularism and propagation of the thought that all religions are equal.

Anyone who used to come to ask for anything, Nanak would give it immediately. But, he never kept an account of it anywhere. The employees of the grocery started feeling scared that Nanak would give away everything from the grocery and run away. If this happened, then Jayaram would be in trouble.

Some courtiers went and complained to the Nawab. He ordered that the goods in the grocery be examined, because it was only on his recommendation and assurance of security, that Nanak had been mad in charge of the grocery. Hence, whatever was the shortage in the accounts of the grocery, he would fulfil it.

Jayaram and some other employees of the court got busy with this work. Everyone believed that the way Nanak Dev had started giving the goods from the grocery to the needy, the goods would have definitely become short in number. But, when each and every item of the grocery was properly weighed and measured, not even one item was short. The faces of Nanak's opponents became pale. The Nawab was very happy. He scolded those who had complained very badly and threatened them that if, in the future, they brought false complaints against Nanak like this they would be severely punished.

Nanak's threat further aggravated the opposing groups' jealousy and hatred. They had been insulted in court. They were not being able to forget it. They started instigating the leaders of the Muslim religion against Nanak.

Nanak had become 18 years old. His parents, sister and brother-in-law thought that he was of a marriageable age. Although boys of 14 and 15 used to get married those days, Nanak had refused to marry. But now, at the age of 18 years, his refusal proved futile and in 1544, on the 24th day of the Hindu month 'Jyeshtha' (June-July), he was married to Sulakshini, daughter of Moolchand Khatri, residents of Babala.

Nanak had agreed to get married only when his father and his in-laws agreed to do so in a simple manner. During his wedding, he broke the religious ceremonies and got married in a simple way. He and his wife took the promise before the timeless fire and said they would keep their relations till the end of their lives.

After his wedding, Nanak continued living in Sultanpur with his wife, and working in the Nawab's grocery. Whenever he would weigh anything on the scale, he would count properly till twelve and then, for thirteen, he would say 'Tera' (Yours) and then, would continue saying 'tera' and nothing else, but, he would measure the right amount.

When the people asked him the reason for it, he said, I only worship God and say "O God! I am yours. All these goods and wealth are yours. I am your trader. All those who come to buy goods doubt that I do not know how to count, but beyond twelve, I do not count. Now who is going to tell that I only sing in your praise? They will be able to understand this only when they also have the same devotion and faith for you." He used to give verbal replies to people like this only. He used to say these words to Bhai Bala and Bhai Mardana during his free time and Mardana used to memorise them and sing them before the common man on the 'rabab'.

There was no shortage of people who were jealous of Nanak Dev. They wanted to somehow remove Nanak from there and place one of their own people so that they could, through that person, take some goods out of the grocery.

But their complaints had no effect. When the calculations used to come out correct, their mouths used to be shut up. But Nanak had come to know from this incident, that their jealousy had turned to malice. He, therefore, wanted to take leave from the grocery. He was waiting for the right opportunity.

It was Nanak's daily routine to wake up at dawn, when the entire city was still asleep and go, along with a servant, to the banks of a river flowing along beside the city. He would have a bath, sit under any tree and pray to God.

As everyday, one day, Nanak woke up early and went to the banks of the river with his servant. The servant quickly took a dip and came to the banks, but Nanak kept going deeper and deeper. The servant, sitting on the banks of the river, kept seeing him going to the middle of the river.

Nanak Dev went into the middle of the waves and took a dip. The servant saw him taking the dip and started washing his clothes in the river. After that, he spread out the clothes to dry. Suddenly, he remembered Nanak. It had been long but Nanak had not come out. The servant got worried. He looked towards the place where Nanak had gone in, but the river was calm and quiet. It was quite deep there. The servant thought it was very difficult for anyone to take such a dip and come back to the surface. He believed, therefore, that Nanak had been drowned in the river.

He went crying to Jayaram's house. When he told them about Nanak, there was a distressful commotion in the house. Jayaram, Nanki and the other members of the household ran towards the river.

In the blink of an eye, the new about Nanak's jumping into the river spread like wild fire throughout the city. Whoever heard it, ran towards the river. In a few days only, Nanak had become so popular in Sultanpur, that in a little while only, the whole city had collected near the river. People started crying incessantly. Everyone was upset by Nanak's drowning.

This included even the people who were jealous of Nanak, those who had complained to the Nawab against him. Those people said that Nanak must have made a lot of mess in the Nawab's grocery and must have therefore committed suicide by jumping into the river, for fear of being caught. There were all kinds of talks.

The divers spread their nets till very far, but Nanak could not be found anywhere. Two days passed. On the third day, one man went to the same place where Nanak used to go to have a bath at dawn. Suddenly, he looked towards the tree under which Nanak used to sit and pray to God after his bath. His mouth dropped open in amazement. He saw that Nanak Dev was sitting under the tree, worshipping God. All around his face, there was a circle of bright light, which made his whole body shine. He kept standing and watching Nanak for some time and then ran back to the city, shouting, "Nanak is alive! Nanak is alive!" His voice echoed in the markets and lanes of the city. People left their beds and came running outside. Nanak's sister Nanki and brother-in-law Jayaram were also among them.

"I had said that my brother cannot die. He has come into this world to show the people on this earth, the path to Mukti (immortal freedom)," Nanki said in a voice choked with happiness, and then she said to Nanak, "Brother, where did you go away? Where did you stay for three days?"

"Sister, I had gone to Sachkhand to meet the formless - God," replied Nanak.

"Sachkhand?"

"Yes, sister. The greatest father, the Nirankar (formless) lives there only," Nanak Dev said: -
"Nirankar lives in Sachkhand.
Let use look at him with gratified eyes
One cannot tell of all his tales
Whoever does, repents later"

Everyone was spellbound to hear Nanak Dev's tales. He also described the beauty there, got up and started walking towards the city.

He straightaway went to the grocery and said, "Take whatever you need."

The crowd charged at the grocery. Whatever they could lay their hands on they took away. Within minutes, the store was empty, as if someone had swept it.

Nanak Dev just swept a glace around the whole store, with a smile on his face. He closed the door and sitting under a tree outside the cremation ground, went into intense meditation. When people who were jealous of Nanak got the news that Nanak had squandered away all the goods of the grocery, they jumped with joy. They went running to the Nawab and said, "Huzur (Sir), whatever we had said is the truth. This time, Nanak has squandered away the entire grocery and is hiding in the cremation ground, due to your fear."

At first, the Nawab did not believe it. But when some other people also told him the same story, he was very angry. He called Jayaram immediately, asked him to take some state officials and calculate how much loss Nanak had caused.

However, when the state officials opened the door of the grocery, they were shocked to see that the grocery was full. When they checked up the goods, not a single thing was missing, as per the list of goods. On close scrutiny, they found that the Nawab owed Nanak Rs. Seven Hundred.

When he was told about it, the Nawab felt very bad, because he had uselessly suspected Nanak. Till now, he had not found such an honest grocer. He scolded the jealous people and told his courtiers to bring Nanak from the cremation ground with respect.

When he was brought, the Nawab said, "Nanak, there is no need for you to get upset. All the goods of the grocery are intact. In fact, I owe you Rs. 700/-." He brought the money and said, "

Take this money and do your work. I will not get as honest a grocer as you."

Nanak replied, "No, Nawab saheb, I cannot work in the grocery of any such person, who cannot give a fist of grains to a hungry person, free of cost. I have not been born to work in your grocery-the formless has sent me to this world for some special work."

The Nawab was stunned to hear Nanak's reply. He asked, "What work has God given you?"

Nanak said, "The formless has sent me to this world so that I can tell the people that they are all the children of the one and only great Father. There is no one big or small, no touchable or untouchable, no Hindu, no Muslim amongst them. They must chant the name of God only, who creates fearlessness and love in them. It removes jealousy and hatred from their minds."

The Nawab asked, "But when did God give you this order?"

"That day, when I went to the Bei River to have a bath, after taking a bath in the river, I went to Sachkhand and stayed there for two days. It was then that the timeless ordered that I should show the world the true path and tell them that we are the children of the one and only timeless man. We shall get salvation only by worshipping Him. Now, I will not work in your store, I will work in the store of God."

"Baba paidha Sachkhand Naunidhi naam garibi payee," meaning Nanak had gone to Sachkhand, where he had got the treasure of fearlessness and the nine treasures (of Kuber-the God of riches).

After saying this, Nanak Dev came out of the Nawab's court and went and sat in the cremation ground. He stopped talking to people and slowly kept praying to God.

Incident of the grocery, of coming out alive even after remaining underwater for three days in the river and the thoughts of Nanak Dev had a very deep influence on the people of the close by areas. People developed a feeling of devotion and respect towards Nanak Dev. They had started considering him as a reincarnation.

Hence, when Nanak Dev was sitting in the cremation ground after adopting silence and worshipping the formless, people used to turn up to have a glance at him.

One day, Nanak Dev broke his silence. The words that came out of his mouth were: -

"There is no Hindu and no Muslim." And then, he kept repeating only this phrase. People used to hear this sentence, but could not understand the meaning of it. Actually, Nanak wanted to imprint this in the minds of the common man that there is no Hindu, nor any Muslim. Everyone is a child of that one and only formless. Difference of Hindu-Muslim is useless. With this small sentence, he wanted to bring people onto the true path. He used to say that there is no true Hindu or true Muslim.

People were unable to go to the depths of these words. Those days, the condition of Nanak Dev was also very strange. His condition had become that of lunatics. He would sit in deep meditation for hours and keep staring into the void. People started saying that the ghosts of the cremation ground had took over Nanak. All kinds of rumours started making the rounds.

Nanki and Jayaram were very worried about Nanak's condition. They tried to make Nanak come back home many times, but they were not successful.

The rumours about Nanak had started reaching the Nawab's ears. After the grocery incident, feelings of devotion, respect and love for Nanak Dev had taken birth in the Nawab's mind. He did not want that an innocent and honest person like Nanak should stay in this condition. Nanak considered that all religions were the same and used to respect everyone who believed in any religion.

After some contemplation, the Nawab called the religious magistrates of the city and said, "Nanak is a very honest and innocent person. People say that he has started living in the cremation ground and the ghosts of the ground have encircled him so badly that his condition has become like that of a mad person's. We do not want that an honest and noble youth like Nanak should lie in a cremation ground. He respects you a lot, because his vision is much beyond the Hindu-Muslim differences. Please go and find out what the actual thing is. What is the reason for his staying in the cremation ground? You please pacify him, make him understand and bring him back."

When the religious magistrates reached the cremation ground, they saw Nanak sitting with the support of a tree. He had his eyes closed and was chanting God's name. His name was all scattered. He had dirty and torn clothes on his body.

"Nanak Dev. What have you done to yourself? The magistrates sat beside him and asked.

When he heard the Qazi's voice, Nanak opened his eyes, looked at him and said, Qazi saheb, some say I am a ghost, some say poor Nanak is a man, Nanak is mad. Yes, Qazi saheb, Nanak is mad, mad about his lord, his formless. Besides him, he does not know anyone. And no one besides that Saheb, knows me."

The Qazi was not able to understand what Nanak was saying. He was trying to understand him when suddenly, from Nanak's mouth came out the words, "No one is either Hindu or Muslim" and then once again, he closed his eyes as before. Hearing the last words of Nanak, the Qazi felt as of Nanak was insulting the Muslims. He said, "How can you say this? We see that there are Hindus as well Muslims in this world."

"This is wrong. Those who are Hindus are Hindus only in name. Similarly, those who are Muslims are Muslims only in name. No Hindu is a true Hindu, neither a Musalman, a true Musalman. They don't posses the qualities which should be there in a true Hindu and a true Musalman."

"If you do not find any difference between the Hindus and Musalman, then come and read the 'Namaz' (Muslim prayer) with us." " Come on," said Nanak Dev and went to the court of the Nawab. After telling the Nawab all the stories, he said, "Today, Nanak Dev will read the namaz with us. Come, you also come with us." The Nawab was astonished. He went with them towards the mosque.

"Nanak Dev was going to the mosque to read the namaz," this news spread like wildfire throughout the city. The Hindus were worried. They considered Nanak to be their guide. If Nanak read the namaz, where would they go? Jayaram had become perturbed to hear this news. Bibi Nanki was not at all worried. She had become acquainted with her brother's reality right since her childhood. She told Jayaram, "You are worrying uselessly. My brother has not gone with the Nawab and the Qazi to read the namaz, he has gone there to show them the right way." And that was exactly how it happened.

A crowd of Muslims had collected outside the mosque to see Nanak going to read the namaz. When they saw Nanak coming, they were thrilled, because the reading of the namaz by a Hindu meant the increase of the Muslims.

When all the namazis (people reading the prayer) went down in obeisance, Nanak too, bowed down, and then, sat cross-legged on the floor.

When the namaz got over, the Qazi and the Nawab saw Nanak sitting on the floor. They were very angry. They considered coming to the mosque and not reading the namaz, to be a big crime, an insult to the religion of Islam.

The Nawab asked angrily, "Nanak, why did you not read the namaz? By doing so, you have insulted both the namaz and the Din-i-Islam. Therefore, you will get severe punishment."

Nanak said, "Forgive me, Nawab saheb, there was no one in the mosque, with whom I could have read the namaz. All the people present here were not really reading the namaz. Each of them was thinking about his problems."

"You are telling a lie," the Qazi said, in an angry tone.

"Qazi Saheb, there is no need to get angry. You are also one of the namazis and you were also not reading the namaz. You were thinking of your newly mated mare and its calf." Then, he turned to the Nawab and said, "You too, instead of reading the namaz, were thinking about buying horses in Kabul."

When they hear Nanak's word, the Qazi and the Nawab's heads bent down in shame. They felt as a repute fakir (saint) was standing in front of them. He understood, without being told, what was happing in the minds of the men. They both bent down at the feet of Nanak.

After coming to Sultanpur, Nanak Dev had been married off. During theses various incidents, on the ninth day of the Hindu month of Bhadrapad (August), in the year 1551, his wife gave birth to their first child. The boy was named Shri Chandra. He was the one who started the indifferent community after the death of Nanak Dev.

After this, in 1553, on the nineteenth day of Phalgun (March), his second son, Lakshmi Das was born. His lineage is famous till today, by the name of 'Bedi'.

Nanak Dev came out of the mosques and went and sat in the cremation ground. He hated the rich and felt sympathetic towards the poor. He would tell the people coming to the cremation ground, the same thing. He used to call the rich people blind and deaf. In one of his couplets he has said,

"Majadhari ati anna bona
Shabad na sunahi bahu role ghachola!"

Meaning, "Once a rich person gets wealth, he does not only become blind, he also becomes deaf, because the voice of the supreme Father, God, is not able to reach his ears."

While staying in the cremation ground, Nanak used to meet the visitors very affectionately. He would advise them to stay away from the share of worldly illusion. He would encourage them to worship the formless. His simple, truthful talks would go down easily into the depths of the listeners' hearts. They would start behaving according to his teachings.

From here only, people started calling Nanak Dev, Guru Nanak. They had started considering him their true teacher or 'guru'. After living for approximately two and a half months in the cremation ground, Nanak felt that the small world of the cremation ground was very small for his purpose. He must leave this small world and must enter the huge and expansive world. So that he can redeem the wayward people and show them the true way. So that he can remove untouchability, casteism and religious discrimination and establish a new society.

He had understood that if one has to achieve the formless, then he will have to wander around from place to place. If he has to obey the order the formless, then, he will have to go to every home and arouse others in the name of The Invisible. God is one, all the people of the world are his children only- to tell them this truth, he will have to go to each person and he will have to give up the limited small world of the cremation ground and go on a journey of the massive world. After deciding everything, he left the cremation ground and came to the house of his sister Nanki, where his wife and both the sons were living.

"There is no point in living here, bebe. The work that the Invisible God has given me, cannot be completed by living here," said Nanak to his sister Nanki.

"Then, will you leave your wife and small children here and go away?" Jayaram became sad to hear this.

"The God that has sent them to this world, He is their actual caretaker. He will only look after them," said Guru Nanak peacefully. "There are many other followers of God, who have moved away from the path of truth. They are loitering around in the jungle of religion, in the darkness of malpractices. The Lord Almighty has instructed me to give them the knowledge and show them the path of truth. I have nothing to do with the false relations and ties of this illusionary world."

Guru Nanak is leaving home and going away - when his father Mehta Kalurai got this news, he came to Sulatnpur to make Guru Nanak understand. Hearing the news even Guru Nanak's wife, Sulakshmi's parents also came there. All of them together tried to explain it to him, but he stayed firm in his decision. They understood that Nanak was not a worldly man. He could not be stopped in any way. They gave Guru Nanak the permission to go.

And then one day, Guru Nanak left his sister's home with Bhai Mardana and started treading on the unknown, unseen path of social welfare.

During that period, a number of evil practices had been born in the Hindu religion. The Brahmin society, which had become very indifferent to their deeds and had given into the darkness of ignorance, was the one to give birth to all these malpractices. In order to feed himself and his family, The Brahmin started propagating many hypocrisies and malpractices. Yet, the simple and the religious people used to consider these uneducated, unwise Brahmins as being of an upper class and superior. Hence they used to do as that class said.

Guru Nanak's mind, from his very childhood, had started remaining sad, because of the prevalence of these malpractices. Slowly, this sadness took the form of rebellion. He decided to pull out and throw this Brahmanism from its very roots. He showed the first rebellion by refusing to wear the sacred thread at the sacred thread ceremony. He told Gopal Pundit:

    Lagu kapahu kateeya Brahman vate Aayee.
    Kati bakra rini khaiya sabhu ko annkh payi
    Hoyi purana sutiye bhi phir paiye horu

Nanak taggun tuhaee tegi hove joru.

Protesting against the artificial yagyopaveet (sacred thread ceremony) he had told Gopal Pundit, "Panditji, I want a yagyopaveet which,

> Daiyaa kapaah sutokhu sootu jatu gandee satu Bantu
> Ehu janeyu jeeu ka hayee te pande ghantu
> Na ehu tute, na malu lage na ehu jaleyee ne jayee
> Dhanu sumanas Nanaka jo gali chale payee.

This means I want the yagyopaveet, which has been made out of the cotton of satisfaction, which has been woven by truth. That yagyopaveet which neither break, nor get dirty nor burnt."

Similarly, when once he had gone to take a bath in the Ganges, he saw many people standing in the current of the Ganga, libation of water to the ancestors. He asked one man, "Brother, what is this that you are doing?"

While giving water to the rising Sun of the East, the man said, "I am giving water to my forefathers, to quench their thirst."

"I do not understand what you are saying," said Nanak. The man explained, "The water that is offered, while facing the East directly, reaches our forefathers, sitting in Heaven. Hence, we have the tradition of offering water to our ancestors."

Nanak Dev's mind was puzzled. He thought, how is it possible that the water we give to our ancestors, reaches heaven from here?

He asked that man, "Will the water really reach Heave?"

"Yes, why not?"

Nanak Dev took off his clothes and went and stood in the current of the Ganga. He turned his face, not towards the East, but towards the West and started throwing water towards the West. The other man was surprised. He said, "Why are you throwing water towards the West and not towards the East?"

"Oh brother, I belong to Punjab, which is towards the West I have fields, which need water. I am trying to quench their thirst." At this the man said, "Have you gone mad? How can your fields get water if you throw water from here?"

"Why not? If the water you offer here, reaches your ancestors in Heaven, then why will my fields, which are just a few kilometres away, not get the water?"

This is how Nanak had tried to uproot the false ideas that people had about religion.

The following is an incident from his childhood. When his father saw that Nanak did not like to take the animals to graze, he thought he should involve Nanak in the work of faming.

"This is not true farming. The Almighty has not sent me into this world to do this false farming," Nanak Dev answered seriously.

"Which is true farming, son?"

"True farming is that which brings benefits in this world or in the next."

"Which harvest is that?"

Through words, Nanak told his father -

    Manuhali kisan hi karni, samupani tanekheha
    Naam beeju santokh suhaga raghu gribi veh
    Rau kam kari janshri se ghar magadh dekhu
    Baba, bhaiya sathi na hoyee
    Iti maiya jagu mohila birla boojhe koyee.

This means, "We must make fields of our bodies, do farming on it, with the ploughs of our minds. We must irrigate it with water of devotion and worship. We must sow the seeds of God's name. We must turn the plank of satisfaction and then adopt humility in our minds, grow the harvest of love. This will bring prosperity to the household. The wealth we earn through the false farming, does not side with us all the time. This time illusion has arrested the entire world. I will do the true farming, whose harvest will give me comfort and happiness right till the end."

No one could understand this type of talk. Even his father, Mehta Kalu Rai could not understand. He started thinking that perhaps Nanak's health was not good. That is why he talked like a mad man, stayed away from children his own age and did not play with them.

He called a doctor and told him everything. The doctor checked Nanak's pulse. At this, Nanak started laughing. In his heart he said, "The Almighty is my doctor. He only knows my actual ailment. He can only treat me. How can you know what my ailment is?"

Nanak jerked his hand away and said -

    Vaid bulaya bandagi, pakad tatohhe baanh
    Bhola vaid na janahi, darad kaleje maanh
    Jahu vaid ghar aapne, meri thaah na le

Ham rache shah apne, tu kis daaru de?
This means, "Vaidyaji, go to your house. You will not be able to find out my illness, nor will you be able to treat it. Only God knows my ailment. He is my true doctor, He only can treat me."
The Vaid heard Nak and went home disappointed.

❑❑

Ever since the journey to Sachkhand, Nanak's condition had become like that of a mad man. He had not attachment left for the world or his family.

One day, he was deep in meditation. Suddenly, he saw a scene enacted before his internal eye. He opened his eyes and hastily told Bhai Mardana, "Right now, when I was concentrating on his Almighty, I saw the whole earth burning. The water of good sermons and knowledge can only extinguish this fire of the earth. The Invisible Almighty has given me the order to try and extinguish this fire. You come along with me."

Bhai Mardana was Guru Nanak's blind follower. What objection could he have? He got ready immediately and Guru Nanak left Sultanpur with him to go out and extinguish the world's fire of hatred, malice and discrimination - a journey that had no destination, no end. They reached a place called Emnabad, where they lived with a poor carpenter called Lalo. Tales of Nanak's fame and reached there before him. When the rich and prosperous people heard that Guru Nanak was living and eating with Lalo, a low class person, they felt very bad. They went to Guruji and asked him to leave Lalo's house and said that they would arrange for his stay and food, but Guru Nanak refused.

Just then, Malik Bhago, a very rich and prosperous person of Emnabad, held a sacrifice and then a massive feast. Hundreds of people from in and around Emnabad came, but Guru Nanak did not go. When Malik Bhago came to know about it, he himself went to Guru Nanak and after a lot of pleading, took him to his house. He requested Guru Nanak to have his meals, but he refused point blank and asked Bhai Lalo to bring the rotis from his house.

Malik Bhago said very humbly, "Hundreds of other people have eaten. If you do not eat, I will feel very bad. You are leaving such delicious food and wanting to eat the dry rotis from the house of a low caste. Why?"

At this, Guru Nanak held a poori, prepared in Malik Bhago's house, in one hand and a roti prepared in Bhai Lalo's house, in the other and pressed them both very tightly. Blood was seen coming out of Malik Bhag's pooris and a stream of milk was coming out Bhai Lalo's rotis! Everyone around was astonished. Then, Guru Nanak said, "Malik Bhago, you have compelled the poor farmers and labourers to contribute the material for this feast. That is why blood is coming out of your pooris. Whereas Bhai Lalo's rotis are made out of the grains cultivated by the sweat of his brow that is why milk is coming out of it. How can I accept such a food which has been prepared out of the blood of the poor people?" Malik Bhago stood there shaking - ashamed and afraid.

"Malik Bhago," said Guru Nanak, "stop tormenting the poor. Whatever you get out of hard work and honesty, be satisfied with that only. What you have, is not true wealth. You get true wealth by serving and helping the poor and the downtrodden, by helping the poor."

"You are right, guruji," said Malik Bhago. He fell down at the feet of Guru Nanak and said, "You have opened my eyes. I spent my entire life collecting this wealth. I considered this everything. But, from today, this won't happen. I shall do as you have said. I shall serve the poor, the weak, the downtrodden and the helpless. It shall be my duty to do so."

When they heard of Malik Bhago's change of heart, everyone present at the festivities started singing praises of Guru Nanak. Malik Bhago was thrilled. He had found a new way - the path of peace and welfare.

◻◻

After spending a few days in Emnabad, Guru Nanak left on a tour of the Western countries. Before leaving, he spoke to his dearest disciple, Bhai Lalo. He said, "Paap ki jhang le kablon dhaya, jori maange dhaan ve Lalo," meaning, "Babar is coming from Kabul with a massive army. He will start rivers of blood here. You leave this city and go far away."

As soon as he had got his orders, Bhai Lalo left Emnabad and started living in a far off village.

After a few days only, Babar's forces fell on Emnabad like a thunderbolt. Thousand were killed. The drains of Emnabad were filled with blood and corpses.

Guru Nanak was going with Bhai Mardana, when suddenly, Babara's forces encircled them and arrested them. They also started protesting like the other prisoners.

One day, Babar's eyes fell on Guru Nanak, who was carrying mud. Babar had a very good understanding of men. He saw this way off hauling mud and stood before him. Seeing Babar Guru Nanak immediately said, "Ek maar payi kurlanhe tai ki dardi na aaya."

When Babar was told what this meant, he released not only Guru Nanak, but also many other prisoners.

□□

One day, while travelling, Guru Nanak reached Mecca along with Bhai Mardana. The long journey had tired them. They lay down under tree on the roadside and fell asleep. Just then, two Muslim men passed that way. They saw that a man was lying down, with his feet towards Kaba. They woke Guru Nanak up and explained to him that he must not sleep with his feet towards Kaba.

Guru Nanak said, "Brother, I can see Kaba on all four sides. If you can, turn my feet that side, where Kaba is not present." Both the Muslim men caught Nanak's feet and turned them the other side. Guru Nanak laughed out aloud. The Muslim men looked surprised. They turned and saw Kaba at the place where they had turned Nanak's feet. Once again, they turned his feet. But again, the Kaba moved that side. Their surprise knew no bounds. By then, a huge crowd of people had collected there. Nanak Dev said, "Khuda, i.e. God is present in every direction and every place. He is in each and every particle of the Earth. What you consider as a marvel is actually the solid truth."

Guru Nanak's words had a deep impact on the citizens of Mecca. They looked upon him as a messiah and started respecting him as one too. After spending a few days in Mecca. Guru Nanak moved towards Baghdad.

◻◻

At that time, a Caliph, who was notorious for exploiting the poor and thereby collecting wealth, was ruling Baghdad. After giving the Arab citizens the sermon of love, peace and goodwill, Guru Nanak reached Baghdad. When the people told him about the Caliph, Guru Nanak, along with Bhai Mardana, went and sat on the road on which the Caliph would pass with his courtiers.

Guru Nanak collected the pebbles on the road under a tree. After some time, when the Caliph was passing that way, he saw the mound of pebbles. He asked Guru Nanak, "What are you people doing? Why are you collecting these pebbles?"

Guru Nanak very coolly said, "When I am dying, I will take them with me."

The Caliph started laughing. He said, "But how will you take them with you?"

Guru Nanak said, "The same way as you will take all the wealth collected by you."

The Caliph was ashamed. There was truth in what Guru Nanak had said. He asked for forgiveness and said, "I assure you that the wealth that I have earned from the blood of the poor, shall be returned itself. You are some leading saint or an angel sent by God."

Then, the Caliph respectfully brought him to the palace. He presented him a gown, which had verses from the Quran written on it. For a few days, Guru Nanak stayed in Baghdad. He delivered sermons of love and brotherhood. Then, he started towards India. The same gown is still kept in the 'gurudwara' of Dera Nanak. Every year, thousands of Sikhs go there, to have a look at it.

◻◻

Those days, Guru Nanak used to live in Kartarpur. He was preaching to his disciples, when suddenly, a youth passing that way came with his friends and sat there. He was so influenced by

Guru Nanak's sermons, that he told his friend, "You go and get a glimpse of the Devi. I will stay here only. When you come back, I will return to the village with you."

The youth belonged to a village of the Ferozepur district, called "Matte ki Sarai". His name was Lahna. When Lahna reached Guru Nanak, he became his only. When his friends came back, after getting a glimpse of the Chintapoorni Devi, Lahna refused to return to the village. This same Lahna became famous as Guru Angad Dev after Nanak Dev. Lahna had immense devotion and faith for his guru. Guru Nanak tested Lahna's devotion many times and then decided that when he was dying, he would give his place to Lahan.

Guru Nanak had reached the end of his life. He held a big sacrifice, for which thousands of his devotees had collected. When the sacrifice got over, Nanak mad Lahna sit on his seat laid his head at his feet and then, announced that from that day onwards, Lahna would be the Master and that his name would cease to be Lahna. It would be Guru Angad Dev. He gave his seat to Guru Angad Dev in 1596 and then, gave up his life.

When preparations for his last rites were being made, his Hindu and Muslims disciples started fighting. The Hindus wanted him to be cremated and the Muslims wanted to give him the grave. Arguing, they went to the place where Nanak's body was lying, covered with a sheet. When they removed the sheet, they were shocked to find, not Guru Nanak's dead body, but flowers.

GURU ANGAD DEV JI

    It happened in 1561.
    A khatri (a Hindu caste) named Pherumal used to live in the village "Matte ki Sarai" in district Ferozepur. He had a grocery shop. On the Pratipada day of Vaishakha, a son was born to his wife Dayakunwari. His parents named him Lahna. He sat on the throne after Guru Nanak as Angad Dev. He was the second spiritual Master of the Sikhs.

As a child, Lahna was extremely good looking. As he grew, his nature proved to be just as beautiful as he was. He was extremely liberal and friendly.

He was still small, when clouds of distress started hovering over Pherumal's head. His village was the property of a Muslim feudal lord. He was extremely cruel and unjust. So, one night, along with his friends and family and his entire wealth, he went to his sister's house in 'Khadur' village of District Amritsar. Pherumal opened a grocery store there.

Pherumal was a worshipper of Goddess Durga. Whenever he used to visit Chintapoorni and Jwala Devi, little Lahna used to go with him. So, from his very childhood, he had a lot of devotion for Goddess Durga. When he grew up, he also started worshipping Goddess Durga every year.

Those days, people used to marry at a young age. Hence, as per the tradition, at the age of 15-16 years, Lahna was married in 1576.

Devichand Khatri used to live in Khadur. His was a well to do family. His daughter Khibi was very good. So, Lahna was married to her.

After his wedding too, Lahna continued his religious works and continued worshipping Mother Bhagwati. Nothing changed. After about five years after his marriage, in 1581, Lahna's wife gave birth to a baby boy. He was named Dasu. Then, Bibi Amro was born. Then son Daatu and daughter Anokhi were born.

Lahna had been religious minded from his childhood. After his father's death, he did take care of the business, but his heart was not at rest. He was on the look out for a Master, who could show him the right path for true peace.

Because of his good behaviour and religious attitude, he received more love and respect than he had expected, in Khadur. People started addressing him as "Chaudhary". There was no shortage at home, but his mind was still restless.

One day, he had just woken up, when he heard the musical notes of Guru Nanak's voice. Nanak's neighbour, Jodha was singing his songs. Jodha was a disciple of Guru Nanak. He used to leave bed at dawn only and after taking a bath, he used to sing his teacher's songs. The words pierced deep into Chaudhary Lahna's heart. He went to Jodha's house and asked, "what is this that you are singing?"

Jodha said, "This is the voice of my Master. My Master Nanak often gives sermons through words called 'shabad'. I am singing that 'shabad' only."

The words and their meaning filled Lahna's heart with peace. He started thinking, "One, whose sermons are so effective, must himself be truly great." He became anxious to meet Guru Nanak. Suddenly, he felt a new light of faith and belief in his mind. His restless mind said that Guru Nanak would definitely remove all restlessness in his inner mind. So, from that day itself, he started waiting for a chance to meet Guru Nanak.

□□

After a few days only, it was Navratri. Like every year, Chaudhary Lahna and his colleagues were getting ready to go on a journey to Chintapoorni and Jwaladevi.

This happened in 1589. At that time, Chaudhary Lahna was only 28-29 years old. He had become the father of two sons and two daughters. He had the burden of his work and family on his shoulders. It is a known fact that the chains of worldly illusions cannot bind one, who has taken birth on this land for the welfare of the people and society. He left Khadur. They were passing Kartarpur, when they saw a crowd of people and stopped there. On asking, they came to know that these were Guru Naka's disciples, who had come to hear his sermons.

Chaudhary Lahna also stood on one side and started hearing it with interest. Each word of Guru Nanak's made him feel as if the darkness was being removed. At the end of the sermon, Lahna felt as if his mind had never been at any unrest. He was felling very light. He told his friends to proceed and said that he would remain there only and join them on their way back to the village.

After his colleagues left, Lahna caught Guru Nanak's feet and said, "After years of loitering about, I have found a true leader. Now, I shall not go anywhere."

Guru Nanak said, "You will stay here only, Lahna and manage the 'langar' (free food)". So, from that time only, from

Chaudhary Lahna, he became Bhai Lahna. When, on their return, his friends asked him to come back to the village, he refused.

◻◻

Guru Nanak Dev had guessed Bhai Lahna's devotion to God and his instincts of service, feelings and duty. With all these, he influenced Nanak so much, that in a few days, he became Guru Nanak's favourite disciple. But, his wife wanted Guru Nanak to give the seat to his eldest son, Shrichand, who also expected the same. Guru Nanak did not want any scramble for power at home. So he thought that through Lahna's actions only, he would tell his wife, sons and disciples, that there was no one more suitable for the Master's seat than Lahna.

It was a cold winter's night. Bhai Lahna used to sleep in the room adjacent to Guru Nanak's room. On the other side of Guru Nanak's room, was another room, in which his two sons, Shrichand and Lakshmichand used to sleep. In the middle of the night, Guru Nanak called both his sons and said, "My clothes have become very dirty. Please take them to the river and wash them and dry them out. I shall wear them in the morning."

Both his sons were surprised to hear this. Going to the river on such a cold night and washing the clothes in the chilly water, was like inviting death itself. So, they said, "We are feeling sleepy. We'll wash your clothes in the morning." And before Guru Nanak could say anything, both the sons went back to their room and went off to sleep.

Guru Nanak called Lahna and said the same thing to him. He immediately said, "As you wish," picked up the clothes and went to the river. He washed the clothes, returned home and dried them. After his bath, Guru Nanak wore those clothes. Later, when his sons came to ask for the clothes, Guru Nanak showed them the clothes he was wearing and said, "There is no need. Bhai Lahna has washed and dried the clothes last night itself." The other disciples sitting around Nanak were astonished. Shrichand and Lakshmichand went back without saying anything.

◻◻

Guru Nanak had a plot of land in Kartarpur, where farming was done. He had cows and buffaloes. Bhai Lahna was given the job of looking after the cattle. There were other disciples also, who used to do farming and look after the cattle.

Once, it rained for many days. When it stopped raining, there was a lot of slime all over. It was not an easy task to get muddy grass in that slime. The fodder had got over. No one was willing to go. But, Bhai Lahna went. When he returned, he was completely covered with slime. But, he did not care. Service had become his main work. Hundreds of his pupils used to come to Guru Nanak every day. They used to keep listening to Guruji's sermons till afternoon. They all used to have their meal in the 'langar'.

Once, they ran short of salt. When Bhai Lahna came to know about this, he went to Khadur and brought a bag of salt on his head. He did not find it insulting at all. One day, after the langar got over, a few pupils of Guru Nanak went there. They were hungry, but the food had finished.

Guru Nanak called both his sons and said, "Please go on top of the Acacia tree and shake the branches very hard. These people have come from very far off and they are hungry. If you shake the branches hard, different kinds of sweets will fall from it. Please feed these to the people." Both the sons were astonished to hear this. How could sweets fall from the Acacia tree? They thought that their father was, without any reason, trying to make them the laughing stock and therefore, they quietly went away from there.

Guru Nanak told his other disciples also, but no one was willing to climb up. But, Bhai Lahna had immense faith and devotion for Guru Nanak. He climbed up the Acacia tree and started shaking the branches.

The people were shocked to see delicious sweets fall from the tree. Bhai Lahna climbed down and fed the sweets to the guests.

□□

One day, a rat died in Guru Nanak's room. Its smell spread inside the whole room. He told his sons and disciples to throw the dead rat away, but it smelt so foul, that no one was willing to touch it. But, Bhai Lahna was willing to touch it. When he was told to do so, he picked up the rat by its tail and went and threw it. On receiving Guru Nanak's orders, he did not care for even the foul smell.

⬜⬜

One day, Guru Nanak purposely threw a bronze bowl into a hole filled with slime and then, ordered his sons and disciples to go and bring the bowl. Everybody made some excuse or the other and went away. In the end, Bhai Lahna was asked to do so. He immediately went into the hole and brought out the bowl. He did not care even a little bit that the slime would cover his whole body.

⬜⬜

One day, Guru Nanak was sitting on his seat deep in devotion. A number of his disciples sat waiting for the prayer to get over. Suddenly, Guru Nanak opened his eyes, gazed at his disciples and then, picking up his stick, lying close by, started attacking all and sundry. Seeing him in this condition, his sons and other disciples started sons and other disciples ran away. But, Bhai Lahna stayed put and suffered the beatings very patiently.

⬜⬜

Guru Nanak had decided to give his seat of the Master to Bhai Lahna, the day he had washed his clothes in the river, in the biting cold.

Guru Nanak had tested him many times. Yet, he decided to give him the toughest test. After acting like a mad man for some time, Guru Nanak got up and went towards the jungle. Many dogs got after him. Seeing him thus, many other disciples and his sons also started going after him. Bhai Lahna was also one of them.

Guru Nanak reached a cremation ground and stopped near a covered dead body. His sons and his followers also reached there. He said, "You have been following me for a very long time. You have come a long way. It is afternoon now. You must be hungry. I will treat you to a very delicious thing." Then, he pointed to the

36

dead body and said, "Eat that." They were all very shocked to hear this. All started moving the other way. But Bhai Lahna went forward and asked, "From which side should I start eating this corpse. From the head or the foot?"

Guru Nanak said, "From the feet." So, Lahna went and sat near the dead body. He removed the cloth covering the feet of the dead body and lo and behold! There was no dead body there. Guru Nanak's face lit up with joy. He became normal again. He went forward and embracing Bhai Lahna said, "From today onwards, you will not be Bhai Lahna, but Angad Dev. I have embraced you. Now, you are my example only."

A few days after this incident, Nanak Dev felt that he would, very soon, have to go from this world. He sent invitations to all his disciples, calling them to Kartarpur, on the 17th day of Ashadh (June-July). Ultimately, the great day came. His court had been decorated very beautifully. But no one knew why. When everyone had collected, Guru Nanak caught hold of Angad Dev's hand and made him sit on his seat and then gave him five paise and a coconut and ordered him to take the mantle of a Guru.

Then he said, "From today, Bhai Angad Dev is your Guru. You will obey his orders only. You have all seen his sense of duty. That is why I have given him my burden." Everyone welcomed his decision, except his two sons. His son Shrichand left home immediately and founded the "Udaseen Community".

□□

Guru Nanak asked Guru Angad Dev to go back to Khadur and propagate his thoughts and principles from there only. So, Guru Angad Dev went back to Khadur. His paternal aunt used to stay there. Her name was Mai Mirai. Guru Angad Dev started living with her instead of living in his own house. He would sit in his room and keep worshipping to the timeless. Three months later, when he got the news of Guru Nanak's death, he came out of the room.

Guru Nanak's disciples pleaded with him to guide them. He accepted this request and used to hold court and started giving sermons to strangers.

Right from the beginning, Guru Angad Dev believed in services, humility and liberality. The words he spoke were so effective, that whoever heard them became a follower.

The fourth and the greatest work he did, was to transcribe Guru Nanak's words and put them in a collection. This is how his words became timeless. These words were, later on included in the Guru Granth Saheb.

Guru Angad Dev had vigour. His thought had influence and power. Like Guru Nanak Dev, even he used to preach to his disciples through words. 63 of the shabads created by him are included in the Guru Granth Saheb.

Guru Angad Dev's voice had a strange effect he used to preach in simple words, about the worship of God. Not only this, he used to tell his followers how they must carry on with their worldly lives, along with the worship of God.

He used to say - whatever has gone to others, he receives that only. It is according to his doings only, that he gets heaven or hell.

In Guru Angad Dev's eyes, work was very important. He became popular very soon, because of his thoughts. Like Guru Nanak, even he objected to the hypocrisy of the religion and the malpractices of the Hindu society. He told his followers to stay away from this hypocrisy and lead a loving life of brotherhood.

Guru Angad Dev's influential voice and his brilliant looks inspired people to free themselves of the religious hypocrisies and the malpractices prevalent in the Hindu society.

Guru Angad Dev did two great jobs. He started the regular tradition of 'langar'. People from all castes and creeds used to sit down together and eat the food. This tradition removed all inequalities and tied all humanity in one thread. He used to say - till such time that the human body is not healthy, healthy or beautiful thoughts cannot take birth in one's mind. If one is weak, one wills neither is able to do any service to society, nor will one be able to help the poor and the downtrodden. So, he opened 'akhadaas', (gymnasiums) in various places and told his followers that the way that they worship and do their prayers every morning, they must also go to these 'akhadaas' and do their exercises. The warfare and the courage that the Sikhs had later, is the gift of these 'akhadaas' only.

Seeing the growing fame of Guru Angad Dev, a sage living in Khadur, started feeling jealous of him. It was because of Guru Angad Dev that people had stopped coming to him. Day and night, he used to wonder how he could get Guru Angad Dev out of Khadur.

One year, there was no rain at all. There was a massive drought. Some people went to the sage and asked him the reason why there was no rain. The sadhu's name was Maluke.

He closed his eyes and sat quietly for some time. Then he opened his eyes and said, "Religion has vanished from the village. Everyone has become so irreligious. It is irreligious to worship a householder." The people asked him the remedy for this. He said, "Till such time that Angad Dev is in this village, there will be no rain. Throw him out of the village and it will start to rain." Somehow, this talk reached Guru Angad Dev's ears. He said, "If my staying here brings a calamity on the people, then, for their good, I must leave this village."

And one day, he quietly left Khadur and started living in a village called 'Tud'. He had stayed there for hardly a few days, when some people from village Chhapri came and took Angad Dev to their village. After staying in Chhapri for a few days, he went to village Bharowal.

Guru Angad Dev left Khadur, but it did not rain. After the lapse of a few months, the villagers went to the sage, but there was no respite.

The sage laughed out aloud and the people understood that this man had hatched a conspiracy to send Angad Dev out of the village, because of his jealousy. The villagers were angry at this show of enmity. So, they beat him black and blue and went to Bharowal. They begged Guru Angad Dev for forgiveness. He had no malice for anyone. So, he returned to Khadur with them.

It was during Nanak Dev's time, that Babar had attacked India and had taken control over Delhi and Agra. Then, his forces kept winning provinces till Bihar. After Babar, his son Humayun sat on the throne of Delhi, but he could not face Sher Shah Suri's army and thus, leaving Delhi, went towards Kabul.

On the way, he found out that nearby, in Khadur village, Guru Angad Dev, Master of the Sikhs, lived. He had heard a lot from his father, about Guru Nanak Dev and Guru Angad Dev's fame had also reached his ears. He told his colleagues to turn the faces of their horses towards Khadur. He said he would meet Guru Angad Dev and then proceed.

When Humayun reached Khadur, Guru Angad Dev was in prayer. For some time, he stood there. He was sure that if and when Guru Angad Dev heard that Delhi's Mughal Humayun had come to meet him, he would stop his prayers. But, Guru Angad Dev did not do so.

After a long time had passed, Humayun got very angry. This was an insult to him. He took out his sword in anger. Just then, Guru Angad Dev, smiling, opened his eyes and said, in a very sweet voice, "You are really a very brave king. Where had this sword of yours gone, when you were fighting Sher Shah Suri? Today, you are raising the same sword at a hermit. Do you want to take out the frustration of defeat, on an ascetic?"

Hearing Guru Angad Dev's words, Humayun felt ashamed. He fell at the Guru's feet and said, "Please forgive me. I have made a grave mistake."

Guru Angad Dev picked Humayun up and in that same peaceful voice said, "I forgive you, king! I know why you have come to me. Go, your desire will be fulfilled. You will get back your lost empire. Don't make the same mistake ever again. A king who does not lose his restraint amidst difficulties never has to witness failure."

Humayun paid his obeisance and went away. After some time, he collected his army and left for the attack on Delhi; defeated Sher Shah Suri and took his empire back after a few months.

Guru Angad Dev never went anywhere. Sometimes, however, he used to go to Goyandwala, where his father Amar Das used to stay.

When he felt that his end was coming near, Bhai Angad Singh called Bhai Amar Das and gave him his seat. And then, on the third day of Baisakh (April), 1609, his spirit went into the Almighty.

GURU AMAR DAS JI

The third Guru of the Sikhs, Guru Amar Das was born on the 19th day of the moonlit fortnight of the Hindu month of Vaishakha in the year 1536, in the Basaar village of District Amritsar. His father Bhai Tejbhanji and mother Lakshmiji, who was also called Sulakshini, were of a religious nature. Their religious thought had their influence on the child Amar Das, right from his childhood. From his youth only, he took interest in visiting the religious places. Every year, he used to go to Haridwar to bathe in the Ganga. This had become a regular habit with him.

As always, once when he was bathing in the Ganges, Pundit Dingaduttji's eyes fell on him. Pundit Dingadutt was a very well known astrologer of his time. He had seen an amazing brilliance on the face of the young Amar Das. He asked him who he was and where he belonged. When Amar Das told him, he studied the lines of his palm and said, "One day you will become the king of some very big state or you will become a very big saint. You will serve the lowly and the downtrodden and achieve a high place."

He was married on the 17th day of Maagh in the year 1559, to Mansa Devi, who gave birth to two daughters named Bibi Dani and Bibi Bhani and two sons named Mohan and Mohri.

Amar Das' father had a grocery store. There was no shortage of anything. Amar Das had everything - a good-looking wife, who was very beautiful, a lot of wealth and all the facility to worship. Yet, Amar Das' mind was restless. A number of saints and ascetics used to come to his house. He was always on the look out for such a person, who he could make his preacher, because he believed that only a Master could show a person the true path.

One day, early in the morning, Amar Das was going somewhere when he heard the beautiful sound of a 'bhajan' (song sung in praise of God). He stood there spell bound, listening. When the bhajan ended and he looked up, he realised that it was the house of his nephew only. He went in and saw that his niece-in-law was singing with great involvement. Amar Das asked Bibi Amno whose song she was singing. She replied that it was a song composed by Guru Nanak Devji. She said, "My father made me learn these bhajans in my childhood only. Everyday, after a bath, I sit down and sing these songs regularly."

Hearing Bibi Amno's words, Amar Das had the desire to meet Guru Angad Devji. He said, "I also want to see Guruji. Will you take me to him."

"Definitely," Bibi Amno said and when she went to her father's house, she took Amar Das with her. The time when Amar Das ji reached Khandur, Guru Angad Dev was giving sermons to his disciples; Amar Das heard him out very intently and then went and fell at his feet and begged him to make him his disciple. So, Guru Angad Dev made him his disciple and gave the responsibility of looking after the langar. At that time, Amar Dasji had become 62 years old. In his Guru's hermitage, Amar Dasji not only looked after the langar, he even served the poor and the downtrodden. He had taken on the job of taking care of all the people who came to listen to his sermons from far and near. He had also taken on the responsibility of Angad Dev's bath. Early in the morning, he used to go to River Beas and bring a pitcher of water for Guruji to have a bath in.

One night, it was raining very heavily. There was slime all around. Amar Das was returning with the water, when his foot slipped and he went and fell near a weaver's frame. But, while falling also, he held the pitcher in such a way, that not even a drop of water spilled out of it. When weaver heard the sound of someone falling, he asked his wife who it was. She replied, "So early in the morning, it can be no one except Amru. He has nowhere to go. Guru Angad Dev is his relative. So, he is living here only." Bhai Amar Das was standing outside. He heard all this. Then he lifted the pitcher and started walking. Guru Angad Dev had a bath with the water he had brought and came to court. He called Bhai Amar Das close to him and asked, "Was there any incident when you were bringing the water from the Beas?"

"Nothing special, Guruji. There was slime on the way. That is why I slipped near a weaver's frame. The weaver's wife took my name and then said that I did not have anywhere in the world to go to, that I was without any shelter."

"No, brother Amar Das, you are not without shelter: -
Tu nithanian da thaan
Nimanian da maan
Nigatiyon di gati
Nipatiyan da pati
Nidhion di peer
Niasayan da aasra
Tum sab da swami"

Guru Angad Dev said this on a happy note. He had been infused with Bhai Amar Das' feeling of service. It was at that time only that he decided that he would give the seat to Bhai Amar Das after him.

One day a man named Gonda Shepherd came to Guru Angad Dev. He told him that he wanted to set up a town named after him, on the banks of the River Beas, but nobody was willing to go and live there.

When Guru Angad Dev asked him the reason for it, he said, "People believe that ghosts live there. They are not willing to go there for fear of these ghosts. If you send any one of your disciples there, then people's fear will go away when they see him living there. I shall get a house built for your disciple and shall serve him well."

"You don't worry. I will send both my sons for your help. When they see them living there, other people will also start living there."

Guru Angad Dev called both his sons - Dasu and Datu and asked them to go with Gonda Shepherd. But, the two sons had heard about the ghosts. They refused to go there, as they were afraid of the ghosts. They asked him to please send some one else. Seeing his sons' cowardice, Guru Angad Dev smiled. He wrote a letter to Bhai Amar Dasji and sent Gonda Shepherd there. He said, "You go to Basarke. One of my pupils lives there. His name is Bhai Amar Das. He is the true successor for the seat of the Master (Guru). Go and give this letter of mine to him." Gonda Shepherd went with the letter to Basarke. As soon as he received the letter, Amar Dasji left for Khadur. He paid his respects at the feet of the guru and asked, "What is the order for me, Guruji?"

"Bhai Amar Dasji, please take Gonda Shepherd with you and help him," said Guru Angad Dev and then, giving him a stick, said, "Take this stick. The ghosts will run away the moment they see the stick."

So, Bhai Amar Dasji and Gonda Shepherd left for that place. Gonda Shepherd started building Goyandwal Nagar on the banks of the River Beas. Slowly, people came and started settling there and soon the township became famous. Bhai Amar Dasji called his family there too.

Guru Angad Dev knew that both his sons were not only jealous of Amar Dasji, they even hated him. Therefore, on the moonlit night of the month of Chaitra in 1609, he handed over the seat of the guru, so that there would not be any fight between the two sons after his death. He also ordered that he'd stay on in Goyandwal and propagate Sikhism. At that time, he was 73 years old.

Both his sons were angry with Guru Angad Dev for this decision of his. They considered it their birthright to get the seat.

So, one day in anger, they went to Goyandwal Nagar. When they reached there, Bhai Amar Das was giving sermons. Both the brothers did not care and started abusing him in front of the whole gathering. Datu kicked Amar Das on his chest and said in an angry tone, "I am the rightful successor to this seat. You get off."

He did not give any importance to Datu's words. He caught hold of and started pressing his feet. He said, "Your feet must have got hurt with my old, hard bones. Let me press your feet." All at the gathering started singing praises of Amar Das' humility. Dasu and Datu's shame knew no bounds. They ran away from the gathering. Guru Amar Das was not in the least bit angered by this insult. But he was upset by the jealousy of his Masters' sons. He could not bear it anymore.

One day, without saying anything to anyone, he left Goyandwal Nagar and returned to Basake. On the door of one room, he wrote, "Nobody should come in. Guru's oath will be on anyone who opens the door and enters." As soon as Guru Amar Das left Goyandwal, Guru Angad Dev's elder son Datu sat on the seat and announced to everyone that Guru Amar Das had nothing to do with the Guru's seat. Now he only should be considered the guru of the Sikhs. But, no one used to come to listen to his sermons. For days he waited, but when no one came, he went back disappointed to Khadur and started sitting in his shop.

The Sikhs were very upset because Amar Dasji had left Goyandwal and gone back. They refused Datu to consider their Guru. After Datu returned, they went to Khadur to bring Amar Dasji back. They included Baba Buddha also. When they reached before the room in which Guru Amar Das had locked himself in, they stopped suddenly and said, "How can one reach Guruji without opening the doors?"

"Don't worry, I will do something or the other, Guruji has only forbidden us to open the doors," said Baba Buddha ji. He made a hole in the wall and went into the room. All the Sikhs were very happy to see Baba Buddha's trick becoming effective. They all went into the room and told Guru Amar Das about the problems of the Sikhs and the miserable condition of Goyandwal.

Mughal emperor Akbar was going to Lahore in 1624. On the way, he met River Beas. Goyandwal was on the banks of this river only where Guru Amar Dasji was staying. Akbar told his commanders, "I have heard that a Hindu saint lives in Goyandwal. People believe he is an incarnation of God. I want to meet him and try to understand the truth about this belief."

One of his commanders said, "Even we have heard a lot about him. In his eyes, there is no Hindu or Muslim. He considers all of them equal. He has a 'langar' (community meal) in his hermitage. Everyone sits down in one line without any difference of caste, religion, status, etc. and eats the food. Guru Amar Dasji also sits with them and eats."

Emperor Akbar ordered the army to camp on the banks of the River Beas and started going to have a glimpse of the Guru ji. He disguised himself and sat on the sides, listening to Guruji's sermons. But the people recognised the emperor and took him respectfully to meet the Guruji. Akbar paid his respects and said, "You are exactly as I had heard about you. If there is any service for me, please tell me." Guru Amar Dasji said, "I am not ordering you, O! Emperor, only requesting you. A true emperor is one who rules over the hearts of his people, considers them equal. You serve the public without any differences. Behave with everyone in a loving manner. Don't misuse your power. You will be benedicted."

The words of Guru Amar Das ji had a very deep influence on Akbar. He promised that he would consider his request, an order and try his best to follow it. He had food at the langar along with his colleagues and came away.

Guru Amar Das ji also, like the other Gurus, gave the seat to Bhai Ramdas on the 13th moon day if the month of Bhadaun (August-September) 1631 and on the 15th day of Bhadaun, left for his heavenly abode. At that time he was 95 years 4 months and one day old.

GURU RAMDAS JI

Guru Ram Dasji, the fourth guru of the Sikhs was born on the second day of Kartik in 1591 in Lahore. His father's name was Harads Sodhi and mother was Daya Kaur. Amidst poverty, Hardas Sodhi was somehow running the household. When Ramdasji, whom his parents named Jethaji, was seven years old, his father suddenly died. A few days after his death, the wife also died, leaving Jethaji all alone in this wide world. He became an orphan.

His grandmother, who used to live in Basarke, took him with them. She used to love him a lot. However, she too was poor. There was no one to earn. So, Jethaji, at that young age, had to work. He started selling boiled gram in the village.

Those days, Guru Amar Das ji was living in Basarke only. Jethaji used to go and sit near his hermitage. He'd sell chhole also and listen to Guruji's sermons.

Jetha ji although poor, had a massive store of the spirit of service. From his childhood itself, he had been taught the feeling of humility, service and obedience. Guru Amar Das ji's eyes fell on him while he was serving at the hermitage. He was good looking, he had a charming personality. It was because of these virtues, that Guru Amar Dasji felt love for him. Whenever there was any work, he would call Jethaji and he'd do it immediately.

At that young age only, he had influenced Amar Dasji so much that when, after taking permission from his Guru Angad Devji, he was going to Goyandwal, he took Jethaji with him too. Here also, he did not stop selling chhole. Whatever he earned, he sent to his poor grandmother.

Guru Amar Dasji's daughter, Bhani had reached a marriageable age. He selected Jathaji and on the 22nd day of Phalgun (February-March), 1610, he tied the two in marriage. Like Jethaji, his wife Bhani too gave the greatest importance to service. Jethaji did not feel any pride at being Guru Amar Dasji's son-in-law, nor did Bibi Bhani feel any pride. They used to wash the utensils, sweep and swab, prepare the water for Guruji's bath and wash his clothes. These they considered their primary duties.

Guru Amar Dasji started getting a well dug for drinking water for the public in general and for irrigating the fields. One day, Jethaji was going to throw the mud, which he carried in a basket on his head, when a group of travellers from Lahore passed that way. Those passengers who knew Jethaji said, "You were born in the Sodhi family. Do you not feel ashamed doing this work?"

Very humbly, Jethaji replied, "Whatever I am doing, is for the service to others. Besides, Guruji's order is like order from God."

This small incident placed Jethaji in a high position, in Amar Das' heart. Those days only, Mughal Emperor Akbar came to the court of Amar Das. He expressed his desire to give some of his property in his name, so that the work of the langar continues in a proper way. But Guruji refused openly. He wanted to keep the arrangements of the langar public only.

The Emperor Akbar gave a little bit of his property in the name of his daughter Bhani, saying that she was his daughter, just as she was the Guruji's and that he could not refuse what was being given to a daughter. These words of Akbar had compelled him to be quiet.

When the well was dug, Guru Amar Das said to Jethaji that he should go to some village in the property and look after it. But Jethaji refused clearly; he did not want to leave Guruji and go elsewhere.

In the end, Guru Amardas told Baba Buddha to go there and he went there immediately.

It had not rained for many years. So, Guruji told Jethaji, "Build a township near a place which is a little lower than the crust of the earth, i.e. where water can stand. Get a big lake dug in that town. It should satisfy the water needs of the inhabitants of that town. Trees can be planted on all four sides of the town. "Alright," said Jethaji and started in search if such a place. He built a town in the land that was given to Bibi Bhani by emperor Akbar. He built an extremely big lake in the middle of the town. He named this town 'Guru's Chakra' but when Jethaji came on the seat as Guru Ramdas, the name of this township was changed to Chakra Ramdas. Later, this came to be called Ramdaspur. Traders from far off places started coming there and started building their business.

It was later that Guru Arjun Dev established a temple in the middle of the lake and named the pond 'Amrit Sarovar'. Later, it came to be known as Amritsar. Guru Arjun Dev made this the main centre of the Sikhs and established the Akal Takht in Harmandir. From that time onwards, Amritsar city has always been considered the main centre for Sikh religion.

When Jethaji established this city and made a big lake, he went back to Guru Amar Dasji. Actually, Guru Amar Dasji had come to know that his end had come near. So, he had called Jethaji back from there.

Guru Amar Dasji had one more daughter. Her name was Bibi Dani. She had been married to Bhai Rana, a disciple of Guru Amar Dasji. But there was a lot of difference between Bhai Jethaji and Bhai Rana. Bhai Rana was proud to be the son-in-law of Guruji. He did not have the feeling of service. Whenever Guruji used to give any instructions to his sons-in-law, Bhai Rana used to ignore them, while Bhai Jethaji used to consider obeying his Guru, his primary duty. Guru Amar Dasji had taken tests of both his sons and his sons-in-law and had found that Jethaji was in every way, suitable to be put on the seat. He called Jethaji and said, "I have tested you a number of times and realised that you alone are capable to take on this important responsibility. I have decided that I shall hand over the seat to you, because you alone will be able to carry on this pure and welfare mission of Guru Nanak Devji and Guru Angad Devji."

Jethaji said, "It is my duty to obey your orders but I am not capable enough to handle such a big responsibility."

"No, Jethaji," said Guru Amar Dasji, "You have all the abilities to handle this post. You have devotion, sacrifice and the feeling of selfless service in your heart. These are not there in everybody. The decision that I have taken is the correct one. Please do not turn it down."

So, on the 18th of Bhadra (August) 1631, Jethaji was coronated to the Guru's seat, as Guru Ramdas. After staying in Goyandwal for a few days, Guru Ramdas Ji came back to Guru Chakra and settled down there only. He could not complete even seven years on that seat. At the young age of 46-47 years only, he gave up his destructible body. It was the teejday of Bhadra in 1638. But a few days before he left for his heavenly abode, he put his third son, Arjun Dev on the Guru seat.

GURU ARJUN DEV JI

Guru Ramdas' wife, Bibi Bhani gave birth to three sons. The eldest was Prithvi Chandra, who was born in 1614. The second, Mahadev, was born in 1617 and in 1620, the third son Arjun Dev was born. This same Arjun Dev became the fifth Guru of the Sikhs. Right from his childhood, Arjun Dev was more capable that his two elder brothers. At a young age only, he had started taking a lot of interest in religious affairs. Selfless service, sacrifice and humility were his greatest virtues. That is why everyone used to love him.

Arjun Dev's second marriage was with Ganga Devi, daughter of Krishna Chandra from Mall village of District Jalandhar. Hargovind ji was born to her on the 21st of Ashadha (7th of July) 1651. He became the sixth guru of the Sikhs. Arjun Dev's first wife had died childless.

The people of Guru Ramdas' family used to live in Lahore. Once, he received the message of the marriage one of his relatives' sons. He called Arjun Dev and said, "Your uncle (tayaji) has sent an invitation from Lahore. I am busy, so you only go and stay there till I do not call you". So, Arjun Dev left for Lahore. The wedding was performed but Arjun Dev's father did not send a call. He would remember him, but without permission, he could not go back to him. He started collecting all the Sikhs living in Lahore. They came regularly to take the Master's instructions from Arjun Dev. He sent three letters to his father, but his elder brother kept all of them with him only. Ultimately, he sent a fourth letter through a trusted person and asked him to give it to Guruji.

Immediately on receiving the letter, Guru Ramdas Ji instructed Bhai Buddha to go to Lahore and bring Arjun Dev with him. Bhai Buddha did exactly that. His eldest son wanted the seat for himself, but because he understood that his father was inclined towards Arjun Dev, he felt jealousy and hatred towards his brother. It became more intense on the Pratipada (the first day of the lunar fortnight) of Bhadra (Hindu month) in 1638, when Guru Ramdas ji gave the seat to Arjun Dev and proclaimed him the fifth guru of the Sikhs. And the same night, he took his wife and few servants and left Amritsar to go and live in Goyandwal. The day he reached there, he left for his heavenly abode.

When Prithvichandra, burning with jealousy, reached Delhi, Jahangir was the ruler. Because he was the only son of Akbar, he used to love Salim a lot. Forgetting his rebellion, he had given the throne to Salim at the time of his death. But, his son Khusro rebelled against him. After being defeated, when Khusro was returning to Lahore, he met Arjun Dev in Amritsar. Guru Arjun Dev refused to help Prince Khusro and said that he would not interfere in government affairs. Prince Khusro went to Lahore with his left over army.

Guru Arjun Devji made a book form of the voices of all proceedings preached and called that collection "Pothi Saheb". Jahangir's chief minister, Chandu Shah, was very angry at the Guruji, because he had refused to marry his daughter to his son. He was looking for an opportunity to avenge this. So, he went to Jahangir and said that Guru Arjun Dev was a traitor, because he had given help and refuge to rebellious Khusro. Those days Jahangir was in Lahore. He called Guru Arjun Dev to his court. Guruji understood that Jahangir would not release him alive. So, he handed over the seat to his 11 year old son Hargovind and said," King Jahangir is feeling scared to see the new consciousness that has awakened in the Sikhs. I may not return from Lahore. Put in all your strength to organise and strengthen the Sikhs. No one has the courage to clash against the powerful and the organised." Guru Arjun Dev left with a few faithful friends.

In a full court, it was alleged that Guru Arjun Dev had assisted rebellious Prince Khusro.

Clarifying his position, Guru Arjun Dev, in very clear words denied helping Prince Khusro. He said, "O King! It is a Guru's court. Its doors are open to all and sundry, all the time, without any discrimination. Prince Khusro had also come. Stopping him would have been against the Guru's traditions."

But Jahangir was not convinced. He sentenced him to death. In 1663, on the banks of the River Ravi, he was made to sit on an iron plate kept atop a burning bhatti (fire) and burning sand was thrown on him. He died sitting on that tray only. He was the first martyr in this story of the Sikh community.

GURU HARGOVIND JI

At the time when, instigated by Prithvichandra, and Chandu Shah, Lahore's Mughal Army Commander Sulchi Kahn brought got his army to put an end to Guru Arjun Dev and then started moving towards Amritsar, Guru Arjun Dev, in order to save the Sikhs from unnecessary bloodshed, left Amritsar. He went to Badal village. Mata Ganga Devi gave birth to a son there. He was named Hargovind. He was born in Ashaadh (June-July) in 1652. He received devotion, service, sacrifice, tolerance and humility as a legacy from his parents. He was the only son of his parents.

Hence, whereas he got immense love, he also got full education and wisdom. He had great love, respect and belief towards his parents. Shri Hargovind ji was born out of continuous devotion for the Almighty and Baba Buddha's blessings. Baba Buddha was no ordinary being. He was Guru Nanak's favourite pupil. He had a firm devotion for Guru Nanak and God. He had served four of the Gurus of the Sikhs. He has a special place in the history of the Sikh community.

The barbaric way, in which Emperor Jahangir had sentenced Guru Arjun Dev to death, had ignited the fire of hatred and intolerance in the minds of the Sikhs towards the Mughal Emperor. The power, with which Guru Arjun Dev had sacrificed himself, had raised a new strength, a new belief in the Sikhs. They got ready to sacrifice their lives for the Sikh religion.

Guru Hargovind was only eleven years old. But, his father's sacrifice, the Mughal Emperor's injustice and the flaming fire of revenge in the minds of the Sikhs had made him mature in his young age. Guru Arjun Devji had given his seat to Guru Hargovindji before going to Lahore, but his formal coronation had not been done. Guru Angad Devji gave that right to Baba Buddha. He only had put the 'Tilak' (Vermilion mark) on the foreheads of Guru Ramdasji and Guru Arjun Devji and finally declared them Gurus.

So, when Baba Buddha started putting Guru Hargovind Sahib formally on the seat, he said, "Babaji, have you forgotten father's sacrifice? Today, besides the knowledge of our scriptures, we also need the knowledge of weapons. It is not long when we might have to raise our swords against the atrocities and the injustices of the Mughals. You gift me the sword."

The entire gathering started shouting out in praise of Guru Hargovind ji. In his intense passion, Baba Buddha put the sword on the right instead of the left side. When he tried to correct his mistake, Guruji said, "Now, let it remain like that only. It will be the sword of compassion." From that day only, Guru Hargovind ji had started carrying two swords instead of one. One was called 'Meeri ki Talwar', the other was called 'Peeri ki Talwar'. On sitting on the seat, Guru Hargovind ji issued an edict that whenever any Sikh comes to Amritsar, he must bring good weapons.

Guru Angad Dev ji had already established the tradition of the wrestling arena. As per Guru Hargovindji's orders, the art of weaponry also started being taught in the arena. Those days, people generally travelled on horseback only. Along with weapons, people also started gifting horses to Guruji. Hence, in a few months only, a powerful army, with 5000 Sikh cavalry was ready.

Guru Hargovind ji married three times. The first marriage was with Damodari, the daughter of Narayan Das, resident of Dalla. She had given birth to Baba Gurditta, Ani Rai and Bibi Veeran.

The second was with Nanki, the daughter of Bhai Harischandra of Bakale. She gave birth to Baba Atal and Guru Tegh Bahadur.

The third marriage was with Mahadevi, daughter of Bhai Dayaram, resident of Bhandiyal. She gave birth to Suryamal. The sixth child of Guru Hargovind was Tegh Bahadur. He was born on the 5th of Vaishakh 1678 to mother Nanki. He was the 9th guru of the Sikhs.

Seeing Guru Hargovind organise the Sikhs into a powerful combatant community, the fire of revenge in the heart of Jahangir's Dewan, Chandu Shah, which had still not died out after Arjun Dev's murder, flared up. Guru Arjun Dev's brother, Prithvichandra's son, Meherban, contributed greatly in accelerating this fire. Chandu shah went and complained to Jahangir that Guru Hargovind had organised a powerful army and collected a store of weapons. He wears royal clothes now. He wants to avenge the death of his father, Arjun Dev. He has got a settee, instead of a seat built. Instead of giving religious sermons, he inspires them to be powerful. He probable wants to establish an independent state.

It was natural, therefore, for Jahangir to become suspicious. He immediately ordered his two officials - Wazir Khan and Beg to go to Amritsar and bring Hargovind with them to Delhi and if he does not agree to come, he should be arrested.

Wazir Shah was Guru Arjun Dev's pupil. He was put in a fire. He could neither arrest his guru's son, nor could he disregard the knight's order.

He went to Amritsar, bowed before Guru Hargovind and said very humbly, "King Jahangir has celled you to Delhi. Please come with me."

Guru Hargovind understood Wazir Khan's dilemma. He accepted his request and on the 2nd of Maagh (January) 1669, started towards Delhi with a number of Sikhs. He set his camp up at 'Majnu ka teela' in Delhi.

On the second day, when Emperor Jahangir called him, he went into court. He was absolutely fearless. He very firmly refuted the allegations levelled against him. Jahangir was very impressed. He withdrew the allegations. He understood that they were all bogus.

Chandu Shah, however, started instigating Jahangir once again. He made the emperor believe that Guru Hargovind's military preparations were an open revolt against the Mughal Sultanate. Jahangir became perturbed. He arrested Hargovind and put him in the fort of Gwalior. Seeing the circumstances, Hargovind sent all the Sikhs, who had come with him, back to Amritsar and asked them to be absolutely quiet.

There were many other political prisoners in the fort. They were the people who had helped Prince Khusro or become the victims of Jahangir's wrath. He was famous that any person, who came into the prison, could not go out, except after his death.

When the Sikhs returned from Delhi and informed the others, not only Guruji's family, all his followers also got worried. They were all well aware of the notoriety of the Gwalior fort. Those days, Lahore's Sufi saint Miyan Mir had a lot of influence. Even Emperor Jahangir used to respect him a lot. He considered him a Godman, an angel in man's form and an honest man, with a pure heart.

Everyone pleaded with Mata Gangadevi to pray to Miyan Mir to speak about Guruji's release. So, when Baba Buddha told Miyan Mir about Guru Hargovind's arrest, he understood that the same way that Chandu Shah had instigated the Emperor and got Arjundev assassinated, he wanted to finish off his son the same way. He assured Baba Buddha and left for Delhi the same day.

In Delhi, he told Jahangir all the things about Chandu Shah's enmity and told him that the purpose behind organising the Sikhs and teaching them the art of war was not to rebel against authority, and that Guru Hargovind was teaching his followers the lessons of devotion and power- both, and that he had not done the right thing by arresting the innocent Guru Hargovind. He further said that there was nothing more shameful than the fact that a Mughal emperor should feel scared.

Jahangir could never disobey Miyan Mir. So, he immediately ordered the release of Guru Hargovind. However, when he heard about it, Guru Hargovind said that he wouldn't leave the jail till such time that all other prisoners were not released. Seeing his determination, Emperor Jahangir ordered the release of all those prisoners also. The Fort in which Guru Hargovind had been kept in arrest, now houses a huge gurudwara. The prisoners who had been released gave the name of 'Bandi Chhod Pir' to Guru Hargovind. Even today, this name is engraved on a platform of the gurudwara. The order for Guru Hargovind's release was handed over to Wazir Khan. He was asked to bring Guruji with him to Delhi. He had released them as per the request of Miyan Mir but was afraid of the growing military strength of he Sikhs. He was afraid that his followers might rebel against him once Guru Hargovind reaches Amritsar. So, he decided to keep Guru Hargovind before his eyes.

When Guru Hargovind reached Delhi, he behaved in a friendly manner with him. He'd keep Guruji with him for hours, even when he'd go out of Delhi. After he had stayed in Delhi for a long time, he told Jahangir that he wanted to go to Amritsar, but he had to go to Kashmir with Jahangir. After that, he could go to Amritsar. Guru Hargovind understood Jahangir's tricks, thought over it in his mind and then went with Jahangir. But at Goyandwal, he told Jahangir that he was going to Amritsar. Jahangir too, changed his plans immediately. He said, "I will also come with you to Amritsar. I shall pay my respects at Harmandir and then return to Lahore."

Guru Hargovind's intentions had been fulfilled. Even if Jahangir went with him to Amritsar, he would not be able to force him to go with him. Jahangir set camp at Gumtale, near Amritsar. He stayed there for a few days then, leaving a small army under the leadership of Wazir Khan, returned to Lahore. He had ordered Wazir Khan to bring Guru Hargovind to Lahore whenever he planned. After staying in Amritsar for a few days, Guru

Hargovind, along with a few trustworthy Sikhs, went to Lahore. Arrangements had been made for his stay in a place called Mujanga. After spending a few days in Lahore, Jahangir told Guru Hargovind, "I am going to Kashmir. You stay here only, in Lahore. My prince will stay with you to take care of you. You may go to Amritsar after I return from Kashmir." Under compulsion, Guru Hargovind had to stay back in Lahore. When Guruji had reached Delhi after being freed from the Gwalior fort, emperor had given Dewan Chandu Shah in his care and said, "He had put in a lot of complaints against you. It was because of him that I had to behave in this way with you. He is your actual culprit. I had him over to you. You may give him any punishment you desire."

When Guru Hargovind had started from Delhi to Lahore, he had taken Chandu Shah with him. He also came to Lahore with him. But insult, anger and jealousy had made him somewhat mad. In that condition only, he fretted and died.

Chandu Shah died, but he left the fire of hatred, revenge and jealousy burning in the heart of his son, Karamchand. He started preparing to take revenge against Guru Hargovind.

In 1687, when the Mughals invaded Guru Hargovindpur, he was within the Mughal army. He, however, was killed while fighting, at the hands of Guru Hargovind only.

While returning from Kashmir, Jahangir died. Guru Hargovind, therefore, came to Amritsar once again, started preaching to his followers. After Jahangir's death, his son Shahjahan sat on the throne of Delhi.

Those days, Shahjahan was in Lahore. Some of the officials of his army came to the jungle to hunt. Guru Hargovind was also hunting with his soldiers in the same jungle.

Suddenly, a white hawk of the military officers of Jahangir fell into the hands of Guru Hargovind's soldiers. Those people had left the hawk to chase some bird.

Shahjahan's hunters came to Hargovind's hunters, while searching for that hawk. When they asked for their hawk, Guru Hargovind's hunters refused to give it back. The hunters of Jahangir were very angry. They told Jahangir the entire story. How could he tolerate any one snatching the hawk of the royal hunters? In anger, he ordered his Commander-in-Chief, Mukhlis

Khan, to get the white Hawk from Hargovind. Mukhlis Khan took 7,000 soldiers to go to Guru Hargovind. To get the hawk back, Guru Hargovind ji got the new of the Mughal attack. He very quickly got a fort built and called it Lahgarh. Here, he appointed 500 Sikh warriors, so that they could stop that Mughal army from entering.

On the 23rd of Jyeshta 1685, Mukhlis Khan's army surrounded Amritsar. For three day, a massive battle continued. Mukhlis Khan, along with many other soldiers, got killed. The small army that was left ran towards Lahore.

In the place, where the Mughal army fought the first battle against the Sikh army, a gurudwara was built in memory of the victory. This gurudwara is known as the Sanglana Saheb.

Guru Hargovind ji knew that this crushing defeat of the Mughal army would increase the anger of the Mughal Emperor Shahjahan and his massive army would get ready to launch a massive attack on Amritsar. So, he sent his family to Goyandwal and himself, went to Kartarpu in District Jalandhar.

Emperor Jahangir had handed over Chandu Shah's property to Guru Hargovind. There was a village named Sahela, near Kartarpur, which was earlier the property of Chandu Shah. But now that village had become 'Guru Hargovind'. He went with his army to that village.

Sahela village's Chaudhary Bhagwan Das was Chandu Shah's special man. He told Guru Hargovind that he could not live in that village. Hence, he should pull out his camps and go away to some far off place. Guru Hargovind told him that his village was now his property. No one can stop him from living in this village. At this, Bhagwan Das' soldiers drew out their swords. Guru Hargovind's fighter Sikhs faced the challenge and killed the soldiers, as well as Bhagwan Das.

To take revenge for the death of his father Chaudhary Bhagwan Das, his son Ratan Chand joined hands with Chandu Shah's son, Karamchand and went to Jalandhar. He instigated Jalandhar's Abdullah Khan against Guru Hargovind and also gave him financial assistance.

There was a massive battle in 1687 with Abdullah Khan. The Sikh army fought the 10,000 soldiers of Abdullah Khan, valiantly, for three days. Abdullah Khan, Ratan Chand and Karamchand were all killed in this war and more than half of Abdullah Khan's army was destroyed. After this war, Sahela village's name changed to Hargovindpur. In 1688, Shahjahan sent a massive army with 35,000 soldiers under the leadership of Beglala to end, forever, the quarrel with Guru Hargovind. Those days, Guru Hargovind was in Kangra. As soon as he got the news of the arrival of the Mughal army, he went to Niyane village. Deciding to fight against them, he set up camp there. At that time, Guru Hargovind had only 3000 soldiers. This war is famous in Sikh history as the war of Mihraj. It lasted for only 48 hours. Beglala was killed in this war and his massive army was also chopped.

The fourth war was fought in 1691. Guruji had given refuge to a Pathan named Paide Khan. He had lived with him for a number of years, but, having been misguided by his sister and brother-in-law, he became an enemy. He came to Delhi and met Emperor Shahjahan and put in a number of complaints against Guru Hargovind. Shahjahan sent 25,000 soldiers under the leadership of Kale Khan, with Paide Khan. Quietly, one night, Kale Khan surrounded Kartarpur. But the Sikh warriors of Guru Hargovind broke the Mughal army's encirclement and killed Kale Khan and Paide Khan.

After giving a crushing defeat to the Mughal army, Guru Hargovind left Kartarpur and came to Kiratpur with his family. Here, he realised that he was fast approaching death. He saw signs of a Master in his grandson, Harirai, who was the son of his eldest son Guru Ditta. He handed over the seat of the Master to Harirai and went to his heavenly abode on Chaitra 5, 1701.

There is one incident of Guru Hargovind's life, which is very interesting. This is proof of how effective his voice was. With his voice, he had made not only Hindus, but also Muslims his followers.

Those days, when he was staying with the Mughal Emperor, Jahangir in Amritsar, a very interesting thing happened. A Sikh of Kabul had heard the order of Guru Hargovind, that any Sikh who comes to visit him, must give arms and ammunitions, instead of other things because he wanted to organise a powerful army of the Sikhs. That Sikh bought a very expensive gift to give to Guruji.

However, when he reached Lahore, he found that Guru Hargovind was there only those days. He started moving towards

Guruji's camp. When the soldiers of the Subehdar (Governor) of Lahore, saw the horse, snatched it from him, beat the Sikh and sent him away. The Sikh went weeping to Guru Hargovind's court and told him the entire story. Guruji told him not to worry and assured him that he would find his horse, but the Sikh said he did not want the horse, that he wanted to see him riding the horse. Guru Hargovind said, "Alright. Whatever you want, will happen." The horse suddenly fell sick that very day. The subehdar called many doctor (hakims) to cure the horse, gave it the best medicines, but the horse's condition, instead of improving, continued to deteriorate. The subehdar was very well acquainted with Guru Hargovind's glory. He decided to gift the horse to Guruji. Emperor Jahangir was very kind towards him. This way, I will be able to please the emperor too and may be, the horse gets cured too. So, he gifted the horse to Guru Hargovind. To the surprise of everyone, the moment the subehdar turned his face, the horse got up as if there had never been anything wrong with him.

The Hindus and the Muslims were both alike, before the eyes of Guru Hargovind. So, there was a very large number of Muslims too, amongst his disciples. They used to come to listen to his sermons, with full respect. He had started the langar daily, because he did not believe in the discriminations of caste or creed.

Those days, Guru Hargovind used to live in a village called Bhujang. In a house close to his, lived a qazi (a Muslim judge who performs the wedding or the nikah). The qazi had a daughter called Kaulan, who was very religious. She considered all religions equal. She used to listen to all the devotional songs sung in the house of Guru Hargovind. These songs and sermons had such a deep impact on her mind that she longed to meet Guru Hargovind. So, one day, Kaulan came out of her house secretly and came and sat in Guru Hargovind's house. She was so impressed by his sermons, that she started coming there everyday and without her parents' permission, took on his tutelage. Her father scolded her by saying, "Guru Hargovind is a kafir. It is a sin to be in contact with such a man. Stop going to his house everyday." But his daughter said, "No one can stop me from going to him. Guru Hargovind is not an atheist, he is the Son of God." Her father, however, did not yield. He threatened to kill her, if she went to Guru Hargovind. Kaulan knew her father well.

She knew that he hated Hindus. She decided to go to Sai Miyan Mir. She went and told him her entire story. Seeing her unlimited love for Guru Hargovind, Miyan Mir went to him and told him Kaulan's story.

Guru Hargovind was far beyond religious discriminations. He did not like the qazi's religious favouritism and obstinacy. So, he called Kaulan to him and the same day, left for Amritsar. He had a separate home built for Kaulan. Now, no one could stop her from listening to his sermons.

So that her name remains imprinted forever, Guru Hargovind had a lake built at the spot where Kaulan used to live and called that lake "Kaulsar Sarovar". Even today, that lake exists as a testimony of this event.

GURU HARIRAI JI

Shri Guru Hargovind married three times and had one daughter and five sons through them. The eldest son was called Guru Ditta. Once, Guru Hargovind had gone to the ashram (hermitage) of the saint Shri Chandra, who asked him for Guru Ditta and had named the successor to his seat. It was from the womb of this Guru Ditta's wife, Nihal Kaur, that Harirai was born in Kiratpur, in Maagh Sudi 13, 1687.

When Guru Hargovind had the inclination that his end was near, then, on the 12th of Chaitra Vadi, 1701, he handed over his seat to his grandson Harirai, who, at that time, was only 14 or 15 years old.

Guru Harirai was married to Krishna Kaur, daughter of Bhai Dayaram of Anup city of Uttar Pradesh. He had two sons Ram Rai and Hari Krishna.

When Guru Harirai sat on the throne, the opposition between the Mughal rule and the Sikhs had become quite clear. The Mughal rulers considered the Sikhs' biggest danger to their rule. Under the leadership of Guru Hargovind, the Sikh army had fought the massive Mughal army five tomes. Although much smaller, the Sikh warriors gave a crushing defeat to the Mughals each time. They had made themselves stronger with the arms, ammunitions and other war goods left behind by the retreating Mughal forces. Just after Guru Harirai sat on the throne, Mughal Emperor Shahjahan fell ill. All his four sins started out with their armies, for the throne. Of them, Aurangzeb was the cleverest and the craftiest. He had taken his two brothers Shuja and Murad, on his side and had pounced on Prince Shikoh, whom Shahjahan had named crown prince.

Dara Shikoh's forces could not battle for too long against the joint forces of these three princes. He was defeated, so he went away to Kabul. On the way, he met Guru Harirai and asked him for help. But Guru Harirai only repeated his determination to not interfere in political issues, like his grandfather and said that he could not help him. Dara Shikoh started from there, disappointed, but Aurangzeb's soldiers arrested him on the way. Aurangzeb suspected that Guru Harirai had helped Dara Shikoh. So, he became his enemy. He wrote a very humble letter to Guru Harirai, requesting him to visit Delhi.

Guru Harirai had Guru Arjun Dev's example before him. The five battles that Guru Hargovind fought with the Mughal armies had taken away the trust that he had on the Mughal Emperor. He understood that this was a vile trick by Aurangzeb. He wanted, somehow or the other, to bring him under his control. One who did not leave his brothers, father and close relatives, could not be expected to be truly friendly towards him.

He said to his eldest son, "You go to Delhi, but be careful about two things - don't do anything which might bring a bad name to the Guru's lineage. The second is that however sweetly Aurangzeb might talk, do not come under his influence."

Aurangzeb was a shrewd diplomat. He gave Ram Rai a royal welcome and praised the Sikh gurus so much, that Ram Rai got entangled in the net. He showed him many miracles. In the end, Aurangzeb said, "In your Guru Granth Saheb, one word of Guru Nanak has been included, in which he had said, "Mitti Musalman ki pede payee ghumiyaar" - has he not insulted the Muslims by saying this?"

Ram Rai did not want to anger Aurangzeb. So he said, "Your Highness, the word of Guru Nanak used in the Guru Granth Saheb, that you are talking about, does not have Musalmaan. It says "Be-imaan" - "Mitti Beimaan ke pede payee ghumiyaar." Ram Rai could not gather the courage to speak the truth. He pleased Aurangzeb but could not control the sorrow and anger of Guru Harirai. Through one of his trusted disciples, he sent Ram Rai a message, that whatever he had done was not correct. It was a big crime, the punishment for which was that he must not return home. If he returns home, he would commit suicide.

When he received Guru Harirai's message, Ram Rai went away to Kartarpur and started opposing him openly. He made the claim for the Master's seat through Aurangzeb, but Guru Harirai and the entire Sikh community rejected the claim. Aurangzeb gave him a lot of property in and around Dehradun, which were not populated at that time. Ram Rai only got it inhabited. Later, it came to be known as Dehradun. In 1708, some Sikhs of Malwa came and took Guru Harirai away with them to Malwa.

In a village of Malwa, lived Roopchand, a disciple of Guru Hargovind. In 1688, when Guru Hargovind fought the third battle against the Mughals, the people of Malwa had sided with him and given a crushing defeat to the massive army of Shahjahan. Roopchand was one of those who had sacrificed his life, while fighting in the battle.

Roopchand had two sons - Phool and Sanwali. Ever since the death of their father, the two brothers had been leading a life of poverty. Roopchand had a brother called Kala. The villagers told Kala that if he took the two boys to Guruji and told him all about them, then Guruji would definitely help them. Kala listened to the villagers and took the two boys to the court of Guru Harirai. As told by their uncle, the two boys started patting their stomachs. Guruji was surprised to see this act of the two boys. He asked, "What are these children saying?"

"Guruji, these children are the orphans of Bhai Roopchand. The father had been killed, fighting on the side of Guru Hargovind, against Shahjahan. They don't have any means of earning even two square meals." Very humbly Kala said, "I give them as much help as I can, but I am very poor myself."

Guru Harirai was very sad to hear this story. He said, "No, these children are not orphans. One day, they will become kings. We shall help them out completely."

When Kala returned and told his wife about the whole incident, she said, "If this was so, why did you not take your own children also? Why didn't you ask Guruji to bless them too?"

Under pressure from his wife, Kala took his sons to Guruji's court. Guru Harirai saw the children and asked, "What is the matter now, Kala?"

"Sir, these are my children. Please bless them too."

"Alright, your sons will be the owners of twenty two villages." Guru Harirai's blessings proved true. Phool and Sanwali became rulers of Jeed and Patiali when they grew up and Kala's sons became the owners of twenty-two villages.

Guru Harirai had only two sons. His older son, Ram Rai had become Aurangzeb's favourite and had started living in Dehradun. The younger Ram Rai was very young.

Guru Harirai had just completed 32 years of his life, when he got the feeling that he must renounce the world. This gave him the feeling that he wouldn't live too long. So, he called all the Sikhs and established his younger son Harikrishna on the seat. He was only 5 years old then. On Kartik 7, in 1718, he left for his heavenly abode.

GURU HARIKRISHNA JI

Guru Harikrishna was the younger son of Guru Harirai. He was born to Mata Krishna Kaur, on Sawan Vadi 10, 1713, in Keeratpur. The name of the son of his second mother Ma Kalyani was Ram Rai, who had been born in 1703.

Guru Harikrishna's mother was a very religious lady. She had been born with the feelings of service and sacrifice and these had been given to her son too. It was because of this, that Guru Harirai had named him the next Guru, at the age of five only. His announcement pleased the Sikhs, but angered his elder brother, Ram Rai. The day Ram Rai had played around with Guru Nanak's words only, to please Aurangzeb, Guru Harirai had extradited him. Aurangzeb had given him property in Dehradun. Ram Rai had full faith that Aurangzeb would help him. So, he went to Delhi and instigated Aurangzeb against Guru Harirai and the small Guru Harikrishna. He told him how his father had punished him, by not giving him the seat, only because he had favoured Aurangzeb.

Aurangzeb was very happy with all this flattery. He felt that if one of his own men led the Sikhs, he would be able to get the entire Sikh community under his control. So, he promised to help Ram Rai. He said, "But how can I dethrone your younger brother, when your father has put him in the seat, with the consent of all the Sikhs?"

Ram Rai said, "You call Harikrishna to Delhi and tell him very clearly, that he has no right to the seat. Ram Rai is older, so he should be the master. He is the eighth guru of the Sikhs; all of them should consider him their Guru."

Ram Rai's plan was correct. Aurangzeb told his Commander Raja Jai Singh, to send a few of his men to Keeratpur, to bring Guru Harikrishna, to Delhi. Jai Singh knew why and considered it improper, but couldn't refuse to obey the emperor. He knew that if he refused, Aurangzeb would send someone else. That man might not give Guru Harikrishna the respect due to him. So, he called his Dewan, explained Aurangzeb and Ram Rai's policies and said, "You please go to Keeratpur and bring Guru Harikrishna with utmost respect and safety, to Delhi. I have obeyed Aurangzeb and told him in no uncertain words, that as long as I am alive, no harm can come to Guruji and that if he tries to arrest or get Guru Harikrishna killed, it will not be good. Tell the Sikhs not to come and that I shall give full protection to him."

Raja Jai Singh's Dewan was a very wise person. He took a few trustworthy men and left for Keeratpur.

Guru Harikrishna had taken on the responsibility of fulfilling his duties at the age of five itself. Although he could not do it himself, his personality itself was so great, that all the work carried on without any problems. It had been only three years, since he had sat on the seat, when Raja Jai Singh's Dewan went to him with Aurangzeb's letter. Everyone present felt worried on reading this letter. They had seen and suffered the results of two letters previously too. Jahangir had sent a letter to Guru Arjun Dev, once and he never returned. Similarly, Jahangir had called Guru Hargovind to Delhi and arrested him in the Gwalior Fort. The hatred that the Mughal Emperors had, for the Sikhs, was no secret. So, majority of the Sikhs advised that Guru Harkrishna should not go to Delhi, because the deceitful emperor Aurangzeb could not be trusted at all.

Raja Jai Singh's Dewan met Mata Krishna and told her that till such time that Raja Jai Singh is there, no one can harm Guruji. And that Raja Jai Singh had given the responsibility of Guruji's security to him.

Guru Harikrishna was only eight years at that time. So, his mother refused to send him to Delhi. The Dewan explained it to her. He said, "You do not know Aurangzeb. If his order is not obeyed, then the entire Sikh community will be endangered. He is very cruel. Hence, it is better that you send Guruji, with me only." At this, his mother gave Guru Harikrishna the permission to go to Delhi.

As they heard that Guru Harikrishna was going to Delhi, the entire Sikh community started coming to Keeratpur. Everyone seemed sad and worried. His mother too, decided to go to Delhi with some trusted Sikhs. On the way, Dewanji took great care of Guruji and his mother. This gave confidence to the mother, that they would not allow any harm to come to Guruji. Raja Sawai Jai Singh welcomed them and took them to his own house. Jai Singhpura was Raja Jai Sigh's personal property. The place in Raja Jai Singh's palace, where Guruji stayed, today houses a huge gurudwara and is called Gurudwara Bagla Saheb. There is a big lake here. It is believed that if one has a bath in this lake and drinks its after, one can get rid of a number of diseases.

After Guru Harikrishna came to Delhi, there was an epidemic of Cholera. People had a lot of faith on Guruji. They started coming to him. Guruji would give them 'charanamrit' (holy water) and they would be cured.

When Guruji was coming from Keeratpur, an astonishing incident took place. There was a village named Panjikhare, near Ambala city. Dewan ordered that they camp there only, as people had got tired, walking from Keeratpur. Dewan decided that they would embark on the journey after three days. A wise Brahmin used to live in Panjikhare, when he saw the crowd of people, he asked whose camp it was. When told he asked who Guru Harikrishna was. When he was told, that he was the eighth Guru of the Sikhs, and was not even eight years old, the Brahmin did not believe it. For he wondered, how an eight year old could have such brains and wisdom. So, he decided to go to him. When Guruji saw him, he smiled, "Come, Panditji." Panditji went to him and said, "I believe you are the eighth Guru of the Sikh community and that you are very wise. I don't believe that any child, at such a young age, can be so knowledgeable." "Then, who can be knowledgeable?" asked Guruji smiling. "One who is well-read, one who has read the scriptures and also meditates and who is older. If you consider yourself so wise, give me the meaning of a few shlokas (couplets) from the Gita. No one can be wise, unless he knows the Gita."

"Does this mean that you consider anyone, who can tell you the meaning of the Gita, wise?" asked Guru Harikrishna. "Yes," said the Brahmin. "Then, it is alright," said Guru Harikrishna smiling. He called Chhajju Jheeur and said, "Panditji wants to know the meaning of the Shlokas. If you know them, please explain them to Panditji."

Chhajju Jeeur said, "As you say." And started reciting the shlokas from the Gita, serially and explaining their meanings. Panditji stood amazed seeing an uneducated man reciting the shlokas from the Gita and explaining their meaning.

Guruji said, "Panditji, wisdom is not related to a person's age or education. The only thing needed is the desire and determination to acquire knowledge." Panditji was ashamed at his failure to understand and his pride and went away from there.

The cholera epidemic in Delhi ended, but soon Chicken pox started spreading. People started dying. They went to Guruji. Earlier, Guru Harikrishna used to give charanamrit to people. But, when the crowd started increasing, he got a reservoir built. Water used to be filled in it. Guruji used to touch the water with his toe. The sick would take water from it, bath with it and drink it too and become free of the disease in a few days. Many days passed, but Aurangzeb did not call them to his court. Nor did he come to meet them himself. Guru Harikrishna was not worried or frightened about Aurangzeb at all. He was prepared to face any challenge. One day, Guru Harikrishna caught the disease himself. He got the blisters of Chicken pox all over his body.

Seeing his condition, a camp was set up at the banks of the Yamuna and Guruji was kept there. People said, "Guruji, you have cured so many people. You can do anything. Cure yourself too." To this Guruji replied, "I can use the powers, given to me by my Gurus, to cure others, but not for myself." As per his instructions, lessons from the Guru Granth Saheb were recited day and night. Hymns used to be sung and the wise men used to give sermons.

Actually, Guru Harikrishna had been badly hurt by his elder brother's behaviour, during his childhood. He did not approve of his opposition to the Gurus and flattery of Aurangzeb. But, he was helpless. He could not ignore his father, Guru Harirai's orders. For a week, he was bed ridden, but the smile on his face never faded. He knew hat his end was approaching, he did not want to trouble his mother, or followers, by talking about his pain.

It was the 14th of Chaitra 1721. It was Wednesday. Guru Harikrishna had stopped talking for many days. His mother and some trustworthy followers kept staring at him, lying in bed. They could see the oil burning out. Some Sikhs folded their hands and said in prayer, "Under whose care are you leaving your disciples? Give us some capable Master, who can show us the way."

Guruji opened his eyes slowly. He asked for a coconut and five paise. The servants brought it. Guruji took all the things, remembered the Gurus and bowed his head before those things. Then, he handed those things over to those standing there and lay down. After some time, he opened his eyes, looked at all the Sikhs standing close by and then closed his eyes again. "Guru Baba Bakale" were his last words. And then, he left for his heavenly abode.

GURU TEGH BAHADUR JI

On Vaishakh Vadi Panchami, 1678, Guru Hargovind ji's wife, Nanki, gave birth to a boy, who was named Tegh Bahadur. Those days, Guru Hargovind resided in Amritsar.

In order to stand up against the atrocities of the Mughal leaders, Guru Hargovind inculcated in the Sikhs, the power along with devotion. He had made horse riding, warfare and the knowledge of arms, an essential thing, along with the study of religion. He had made arrangements to teach the use of arms along with religion, for his own sons too. Tegh Bahadur had, in comparison to his other brothers, learnt of warfare and the direction of arms in a much shorter time.

His mind, however, was in the worship of God. He used to spend hours, in prayer. At that time only, the Mughal army invaded Keeratpur. At a small age only, Tegh Bahadur showed such valour, that the renowned warriors were astonished. He was married at the age of thirteen years, to Gujri, daughter of Lalchand, a resident of Kartarpur. He left Keeratpur and started living in Baba Bakale. It was here, in isolation, that he started worshipping God.

After the death of Guru Harikrishna many people of the Sodhi family, besides Ram Rai and Dheermal, proclaimed themselves the Gurus. Because at the last moment, Guru Harikrishna had said, "Baba Bakale". So, they all came and set camp there. They would all hold forth and give sermons. All the six came to Bakale in searched a teacher. They would listen to all of them, but could not decide who the actual Guru was.

Those days, there was a trader called Makkhan Shah Lubana. He had trade with various foreign countries. Once, one of his ships, carrying his goods, got caught in a sea storm. People in the ship started feeling scared that the ship might drown. Makkhan Shah was a devotee of Guru Nanak Devji. When he heard the wails of women and children, he started remembering Guru Nanak and vowed that if his ship came out safe from the storm, he would offer five hundred gold coins to the seat of the Gurus. Even before he could complete his prayer, his ship went and stood near an island. Makkhan Shah reached home safely and started looking for the Guruji. He heard that Guru Harikrishna had died and the new Guru was in Bakale. There, he saw 22 people who were claiming to be the Gurus.

Makkhan Shah was a clever trader. He thought he'd give five gold coins to each Guru. Whoever is the true Guru, he would ask for the rest of the coins too. He did that, but no one asked for the rest of the coins. Disappointed, Makkhan Singh asked, "Does anyone else form the family of the Gurus live in Bakale?" People told him that Guru Hargovind's son, Tegh Bahadur, was living in a cave. Makkhan Shah went there. He waited for Tegh Bahadur to finish his prayers. Makkhan Shah put five coins at his feet too. At this, Tegh Bahadur said, "Makkhan Shah, look at my back."

Makkhan Shah saw the wounds that had been made by the piercing of nails. Blood was flowing out of them.

Shri Tegh Bahadur said, "When your ship was about to drown, you had promised to offer five hundred coins. Now, you are showing only five?"

Hearing Tegh Bahadur's words, Makkhan Shah's joy knew no bounds. He climbed on the roof of the cave and started shouting, "The Guru has been found - the Guru has been found."

People came running. When they were told of the entire episode, people accepted Tegh Bahadur, son of Guru Hargovind, as the actual successor to the Gurus' seat. This message was sent far and wide. The whole of Bakale started reverberating to the sounds of welcoming Guru Tegh Bahadur.

Dheermal saw all this and started burning with anger. He, along with some of his people, attacked Tegh Bahadur's house and stole the money, etc. that his followers had given as gift. When Makkhan Shah came to know about it, he, along with his servants, encircled the house of Dheermal. The news that a new Guru had been found, reached Delhi too. Those Sikhs, with whom Guru Harikrishna had left the coconut and the five paise, also came there. In a short time, all the Sikhs from the far off places also reached there. And on Chaitra Sudi 14, 1721, Tegh Bahadur was traditionally placed on the Gurus' seat.

After spending a few days in Bakale, Guru Tegh Bahadur, along with Makkhan Shah and the other Sikhs, went to Amritsar. They wanted to visit Harmandir, but the self-appointed priest of Harmandir, Haiji Sondhi, got the doors closed. He was afraid that Guru Tegh Bahadur might establish his control on the mandir and he would have to go away and therefore lose the income from the daily offerings.

When his associates suggested that they get the doors of the mandir opened forcibly, Guru Tegh Bahadur refused and went to Balla village near Amritsar. He lived on a platform under a berry tree. In memory of that, a gurudwara had been built there. It is called Gurudwara Thada Saheb. Another gurudwara called Gurudwara Kotha Saheb was built in the Balla village.

After spending a few days in Balla, Guru Tegh Bahadur returned to Bakale, but the people of his family, who considered themselves the successor to the seat, stared troubling him. Guru

Tegh Bahadur decided to tour the whole of India and spread the message of Guru Nanak throughout the length and breadth of the country. He reached Bhagowal village in Kaltur province. This village is in the lap of the mountains. Seeing the beauty all around, he bought the village from the king and set up the city of Anandpur. This is the same Anandpur that was later made the capital by Guru Govind Singh. After spending 6 months here, he proceeded further. He went to Delhi, Mathura, Vrindavan, Agra, Etawah, Kanpur and finally reached Prayag. After staying here for six months, he went to Patna. Those days, Mata Gujri was pregnant. So, Guru Tegh Bahadur decided to stay on in Patna. Fortunately, a businessman of Patna was so impressed by Guru Tegh Bahadur that he gave away his mansion (haveli) of Atamganj, to Guruji. Guru Tegh Bahadur left his family there and went on ahead. He toured Dacca and Assam too and returned to Patna after four years. In the meantime, his wife had already given birth to a son. He was named Govind.

During Guru Tegh Bahadur's Assam tour, two important incidents took place. There was a state called Cooch Bihar, which spread till Assam. Earlier, it used to bring a huge amount as taxes for the government. But, suddenly, the king stopped paying the tax. Emperor Aurangzeb sent his men to collect the tax two or three times, but the king refused to pay point blank. Not only this, they even killed some of them and some escaped.

When the escaped ones went and told Aurangzeb, he was furious. He sent a large army under the commandership of Sawai Raja Ram Singh, son of Maharaja Sawai Jai Singh of Jaipur. He ordered that Cooch Bihar be brought and added on to the Mughal Sultanate (empire). If the king survived, he should be arrested and presented before the Delhi Durbar.

Those days, Guru Tegh Bahadur was in Assam only. The king of Assam had welcomed him and made all the preparations to keep him like a State guest.

The king of Assam did not have any son. When he came to know of Guru Tegh Bahadur's greatness, he went to him and told him his tale of woe. Guruji blessed him and said, "There is no need to be sad. You will not be childless. A son will soon be born in your house." After sometime, the queen gave birth to a boy. The king named him Ratna Rai. By the time this boy grew up and learnt that he had been born with the blessings of Guruji, Guru Tegh Bahadur had already died. He took many elephants and five invaluable things and went to Anandpur. He placed all these things at the feet of Guru Govind Sign ji. Guru Govind Singh has made a mention of it, in his "Vichitra Jeevan".

Sawai Raja Ram Singh set camp in Guwahati, across the River Brahmaputra and awaited Guru Tegh Bahadur's return from Dacca. As soon as Tegh Bahadur got the message, he left Dacca and set camp at a town called Ghuvdi, on the other side of River Brahmaputra. Sawai Raja Ram Singh came to Ghuvdi to seek his blessings.

It was a small town of Cooch Bihar. The ruler got scared to see such a huge army (as the one with Sawai Raja Ram Singh) and when he heard that even Guru Tegh Bahadur was with the Mughal Commander, he lost all hope. He understood that he could not fight the army, which had the support of Guru Tegh Bahadur. After a lot of contemplation, he went to Guru Tegh Bahadur and asked him to save him from the wrath of the Mughal Emperor Aurangzeb. Guru Tegh Bahadur was a peace loving man. He did not want that so many people should be killed. So, he convinced Raja Ram Singh to form a treaty mutually, but when the question of determining the limits came, both stuck to what they felt was right. At this, Guru Tegh Bahadur drew out his sword and jumped high and the sword fell on the ground. That, he said, was the limit of the two States. Both accepted it and a massacre of thousands was averted.

□□

Travelling from Assam, through many states of Bengal, Guru Tegh Bahadur reached Patna. His son, Govind, had become four years old. Whenever Guru Tegh Bahadur looked at his son, he understood that he had, at last, found his actual successor. He stayed in Patna for some time. The whole country was groaning under the atrocities of Emperor Aurangzeb. He not only levied improper taxes on the Hindus, he even razed to the ground, their temples and got mosques built. He forced them to convert to Islam. Not only their religion, but also even the lives of the

Hindus, landed in trouble. The condition of Punjab and Kashmir had become very pitiable. Beautiful women were unsafe.

Guru Tegh Bahadur had left Punjab many years back, but news of Aurangzeb's atrocities had reached him. So, he decided to come to Punjab. Because Sawai Raja Ram Singh was with him, they did not object to his going to Punjab. As before, Guru Tegh Bahadur started setting court every day. The atmosphere in Anandpur became peaceful. So, he called his family to Delhi.

Suddenly, one day, some Kashmiri Brahmin people came to him and said, "We are coming from Kashmir. The property of all Hindus, their lives and their religion are in danger. Now, only you can redress our woes. You know Aurangzeb and his anti-Hindu policies. He has ordered Sher Afghan, the Subehdar of Kashmir, to convert forcefully, all Hindus, to Islam. Any one who refuses may be done to death. The Sikh Gurus have always protected Hinduism with their support. We pray to you to protect us from disaster."

Hearing this from the Kashmiri Pundits, Guru Tegh Bahadur fell into deep thought. Aurangzeb was the ruler of the country. Guru Tegh Bahadur did not like the ruler's policy of favouring one religion and getting the people of another religion converted forcibly. Right from the time of Guru Nanak, no Guru had laid emphasis on religious discrimination. For them, all religions were equal. Guru Tegh Bahadur was very well acquainted with the condition of the country. He assured the Kashmiri Pundits and said, "Go back home, without any worry. Now, if Sher Afghan forces you to get converted, tell him fearlessly that if Guru Tegh Bahadur accepts Islam, you will too." And they returned home.

□□

After a few days, Subehdar Sher Afghan sent his soldiers to call the Pundits. He started forcing them to become Muslims. The Pundits fearlessly said, "If the ninth Guru of the Sikhs, Guru Tegh Bahadur agrees to become a Muslim, we also will agree." When he heard this reply, Sher Afghan became very angry. He immediately sent a long letter to Aurangzeb, saying that Guru Tegh Bahadur was creating problems in the way of conversions and that this was a direct revolt against the royal order. Hence,

Guru Tegh Bahadur must be given severe punishment, so that he may stop putting hurdles in the way of Islam. He has told the people that they can covert to Islam if he accepts it. So, he must be forced to accept Islam.

Aurangzeb used to consider Guru Tegh Bahadur to be an enemy of Islam. He had wanted to spread Islam. He was a staunch Muslim and had decided that he would, very soon, turn the whole of India into a Muslim State. He knew that if Guru Tegh Bahadur became a Muslim, all is followers would also accept Islam. So, he sent his army to bring Guruji to Delhi, somehow or the other. Guru Tegh Bahadur called his people, told them about Aurangzeb and said, "The time has come for some divine soul to sacrifice himself for the protection of the Hindu religion." His son, Govind Rai, who was sitting close to him, said, "Father, who in this county, at this time, has a more divine soul than your?" Admiringly, Guru Tegh Bahadur looked at his son and said, "You are right, son. For the sake of the religion, I shall sacrifice my life. I am going to Delhi. Now, Govind Rai only will finish my incomplete work. You may put him on the seat at an auspicious time."

He appointed a few of his followers to look after Govind Rai and carry on the work of the panth and one day, he took ten of his faithful friends and left for Delhi. Those days, Aurangzeb was in Agra. So, Guru Tegh Bahadur decided to go to Agra. On the way, he stopped at Ropar. Ropar's Pathan ruler was his devotee. He gave him a warm welcome and took him to his fort. When he came to know that Guruji was going to Agra, to meet Aurangzeb, he said that he would not let him go. He said, "Aurangzeb is cruel and deceitful. He will treat you the way Jahangir treated Guru Arjun Dev. You stay here only. Till such time that I or any member of my family is alive, Aurangzeb will not be able to harm you." But Guru Tegh Bahadur quietened him by saying that the time had still not come, then, he went to Agra. He asked five of his followers - Bhai Matidas, Bhai Guru Ditta, Bhai Dayala, Bhai Uda and Bhai Chimaji - to remain with him and sent the other five to Punjab. He started living with his five followers in a place, which was five miles away from Agra. The 'kiladar' (caretaker of the fort) got the news. So he went and arrested Guruji and his five followers and brought them to Agra and after a few days, sent them to Delhi.

◻◻

When they reached Delhi, they were kept under house arrest. They could neither go out of the haveli (bungalow) nor could any one go to see them. Aurangzeb sent some army officials and qazis (religious lawyers) to ask Guru Tegh Bahadur to accept Islam, but he refused saying, "I can give up my life, but not my religion. Although in my eyes, all religions are equal." They tried to tempt his followers in every possible way, but they refused. Disappointed, the qazi went back. When Aurangzeb hear Guru Tegh Bahadur's reply, he was furious. He ordered that an iron cage be made and placed in front of the Chandni Chowk Police Station and Guru Tegh Bahadur be imprisoned inside it. Then, before his eyes, his five disciples should be beaten so badly, that in fear of death, they would be compelled to accept Islam. The cage made for Guruji was so small that he could neither stand nor lie down. He could only sit. The cage was placed right in the centre of Chandni Chowk.

The qazis went to Bhai Matidas and told him that if he accepts Islam, then he'd be married to some nawab's daughter. He would be made the subehdar of some province. Otherwise, he'd be given such a deadly punishment that even death will feel scared. Bhai Matidas laughed loudly and said, "What else can be expected from cruel people like you. You may chop my body to pieces but you can't make me change my religion."

"Alright, I give you the whole night to think. If you refuse in the morning also, then we will saw your body into two parts."

◻◻

The next day, the qazi came to Bhai Matidas once again. But he repeated what he had said earlier. An announcement for the threat was made and majority of the Delhi population came to see Aurangzeb's live example. Bhai Matidas was brought out onto the platform, but he stuck to his earlier response. The people came with saws and put them on his head. The main qazi said,

"Matidas, what is your last wish?" "I have only one desire," Bhai Matidas said, "I should be made to sit in such a way that when you saw me, my face is towards my Guru. I want to die looking at him." This request of Bhai Matidas was granted. He continued to pray peacefully. Soon, his body was cut into two pieces.

Guru Tegh Bahadur kept watching his favourite pupil being sacrificed. This was the first time, after Guru Arjun Dev that a Sikh had given up his life for the Hindu religion.

□□

The next day, the qazi went to Bhai Dayala. They gave him the same offers but he too fearlessly refused, like Matidas.

The next day, on the same platform, a huge fire was made. A huge vessel of copper was placed on it and Bhai Dayala was made to stand in it. The vessel was so huge that after standing in it, only his shoulders and head were visible. Then water was filled into it and the fire was lit. The water started boiling. Bhai Dayala saluted his Guruji in the cage across the stream and started doing his prayers. In a short time, Bhai Dayala's full body was boiled.

Seeing Bhai Matidas and Bhai Dayala being sacrificed like this, Bhai Uda and Bhai Chimaji thought instead of dying like this, it would be better to die fighting the enemy. They expressed their thoughts to Guruji. He gave them permission to run away, if they could. The same night, the two escaped and ran to Anandpur. Only Bhai Guruditta was left with his Guruji.

□□

The next day the qazi went to Guru Tegh Bahadur and tried to make him understand. But, Guruji said, "I can give my head, not my religion. The next day, in front of the police station, where stands Gurudwara Sheeshganj, Guru Tegh Bahadur was brought and made to sit on the platform. The slaughterer set eyes on Guruji's neck and struck his sword so hard that his head separated from his body in one strike only. Both- his body and his head were left lying there only to frighten the people so that they'd accept Islam themselves.

The moment Guruji's head was chopped off there was chaos. People started running helter shelter. In that confusion, two Sikhs reached that place. One of them was Bhai Jaita. He picked up Guruji's head, covered it in a sheet and took it to Anandpur. He gave the head to Guruji's son, Govind Rai who cremated it as per the rites.

Lakkhishah Banjara picked up the body and hid it in a cart, full of hay and took it to the place where today, Gurudwara Rakabganj stands. He lit fire to a hut there and consigned Guruji's body to the flames.

The entire nation was shocked by Aurangzeb's cruelty.

GURU GOVIND SINGH JI

The sacrifice of Guru Tegh Bahadur and his disciples had shaken the entire nation. A volcano of hatred had erupted in the minds of the Hindus, towards the Mughal rule. Instead of the Mughal regime, the Mughal rulers started being opposed. The sons, Govind Rai, who became the tenth guru of the Sikhs, added the word 'Singh' with the names of the Sikhs. Instead of Guru Rai, he started being called Guru Govind Singh. He was determined to form the Sikh community into a warrior and brave community to take revenge for the merciless killings of his father and the other

Sikhs. He drilled it into the minds of the Sikhs that one Sikh was equal to a lakh and 25 thousand Mughal soldiers. He combined belief and devotion with power. He brought such realisation along with rebellion in the country that shook the roots of the Mughal regime. As a result, all the provinces of the Mughal Empire started dreaming of freedom. The Hindu Kings started building their strength.

The tenth and last guru of the Sikhs, Guru Govind Singh was born on the Paush Sudi Saptami 1723, i.e. December 22, in Patna in Bihar.

At the time when Guru Tegh Bahadur was journeying from the West to the East propagating Sikh ideology; he had left his wife Gujri and mother Nanki in Patna. He had appointed some man to look after them.

At the time that Guru Govind Rai was born, Guru Tegh Bahadur was in Assam. After touring the holy places and various towns in Assam and Bengal, when Guru Tegh Bahadur reached Patna, his son Govind Rai had become four years old.

From his childhood only, Govind Rai's nature was different from that of the other children. At an age when children play with toys, he played with swords, daggers, bows and spears. When he started walking, i.e. when he became three years old, he started making warriors of his friends and divided them into the two armies. He became the commander of one army and would fight a war with the soldiers of the other army.

Right from his childhood, he was very apt at shooting arrows. Outside his houses was a well, from where the women of the neighbourhood used to fill water. Govind Rai would hide in some places. As soon as the woman would fill her pitcher, he'd shoot it down with his arrows. The woman came and complained about it to Mata Gujri, who gave them brass pitchers, because Govind Rai started targeting them too.

There is a gurudwara in Patna called Bhaini Saheb. Baby Govind Rai's small 'khadaun' (wooden slippers), clothes, spear and small bow and arrow are still kept there.

While staying in Patna only, the child Govind Rai received education in Sanskrit and Persian. After Guru Govind Sigh made arrangements for his education in Anandpur, he received complete education in Sanskrit, Arabic, Persian and Gurmukhi.

When the Kashmiri Pandits, tired of Aurangzeb's atrocities, came to Guru Tegh Bahadur and told him of their tale of woe, Guruji said, "The head of some great man is needed." At this, Guru Govind Rai, unhesitatingly replied, "There can be no greater person in this world, than you." at that time, he was only 9 years old. Nowhere in the history of the world, has it been heard that a son inspires his father to give up his life, for the sake of his religion. He was made to sit on the seat on Vaishakh 3, 1733.

When he was living in Patna, Govind Rai was only 4 years old. People started considering him to be God's reincarnation.

Bheekhan Shah, who lived in Gudak village of Patida state, was the one who realised this first. When Guru Govind Singh was born, Bheekhan Shah had felt that some Godly power had been born in Patna. And the moment he felt this, he left for Patna.

After completing the long and tiring journey, when he reached the house of Guru Govind Singh, his head automatically bent down before him. He placed two bowls in front of him. One had milk and the other had water. He had meant the bowl of milk to represent the Hindu religion and the bowl of water to represent the Deen-i-Islam. By keeping both the bowls in front of him, he wanted to know whose side Guru Govind Singh would take when he grew up. In his mind, he had decided that Guruji would kick whichever he wanted to oppose. Bheekhan Shah's surprise knew no bounds when Govind kicked both the bowls. It was clear that he would consider both the religions equal. He had put his head on Govind's feet and predicted that "This child is no ordinary child. He has a divine light. No one will be able to match his bravery. He has taken birth to help the needy and destroy the tyrannous."

❏❏

A very wealthy and prosperous man used to live in Patna. His name was Raja Fatehchand. He had everything, except a child. So, both husband and wife used to be very sad. They gave charity, visited holy shrines, worshipped and did all kinds of things, but nothing helped. Suddenly, someone told them about this remarkable boy, who was the son of Guru Tegh Bahadur, the Guru of the Sikhs. He told them that they must visit him for their wishes may be fulfilled. So, the two went to him and told Mata Gujri, the wife of Guru Tegh Bahadur, the whole story. She called Govind Rai and asked him to do so. He smiled at the queen and said, "Mother, they have many boats. First they must take me boating. Only than will their desire be fulfilled." Raja Fatehchand was thrilled and said that he would do so. Govind Rai climbed down from his mother's lap and, picked up a stick lying close by, touched it to the Rani's head and said, "She will not have one, but five sons." And then, he ran away to play with his friends. Soon, the Rani gave birth to her first son. They became his disciples for life. Even after Govind Singh left Patna and started living in Anandpur, they came to visit him.

□□

There was a scholar named Shivdatt also in Patna. He was a devotee of Ram. The child Govind used to go to bath at the same bank that he used to bath and meditate in. One day, when he went for his bath, he saw Govind Rai, deep in meditation. He had already heard of all his miracles. When Govind Rai opened his eyes, he saw Pandit Shivdutt. He smiled, paid his obeisance to him and said, "Please tell me if I could be of any service to you," Panditji said, "Your miracles are famous in the entire city. People consider you a reincarnation of God. But, I do not believe it. If you can, show my God Ram to me. I will also starts considering you a great man." Govind Rai said, "Panditji, I do not know what a miracle is and what people say about me, but if you want to see your God, close your eyes." He closed his eyes. Suddenly, he felt a mass of light on his eyelids. This mass grew bigger and bigger into the image of Lord Ram, that he worshipped him in. Then, this mass became smaller and smaller and ultimately, went into the child Govind.

□□

From his very childhood, Govind was distant from worldly entanglements. Once, Mata Gujri made him wear gold bangles. After a few days she saw that the bangle of one hand, was missing. When asked, he said that it had got lost just then. She got worried and asked, "Where did you lose it? It was very expensive. Take me to the place where you were playing. Maybe it fell down there." So, they both went to the banks of the River Ganga. He took off the other bangle, threw it into the Ganga and said, "Mother, that bangle got lost there." When his mother said, "What did you do? You threw the other bangle too!" Govind Rai said, "Mother, after throwing the bangle, I am feeling free. You had chained me up. If I get chained, then I will not be able to tread on the path shown by Guru Nanak Devji and my father." Hearing such words from a three-year-old child amazed Mata Gujri. Then, he hugged and caressed him.

☐☐

As soon as he became the Guru, Govind Singh started giving the Sikhs the education of power, along with literary education. He started making an effort to remove the inferiority complex that the Hindu psyche was suffering from. He soon organised an army that would stand as a hurdle in the oath of Mughal atrocities and would awaken the Hindu society. He asked his followers to wear arms, so that when the need arises, they can protect themselves and others.

He got good horses, from Kabul and encouraged the Sikhs to gift horses instead of any other material thing. He soon gave Anandpur, the form of a cantonment. He got a strong wall built around the city and converted his house into a fort. He also made a nagara (drum), which he called, the Ranjit nagara, whose sound could be hear miles away. As soon as they heard these sounds, Sikhs with arms, would come riding in. He named his army, "Sant Sena". He encouraged every young and healthy person to join this army. Soon his followers in Kabul, Kandahar, Gazni and Bokhara started gifting horses to him. He told his men to be alert all the time, as there could be a war anytime. The army vowed to give up their all, to protect the country and the religion.

It was the auspicious time of Baisakhi, in 1756. Sikhs from all over the country were collecting in Anandpur. Their clothes, language, customs, were all different, but their aim was one, their thoughts were one, they were all tied by one promise. The way their Guru, Guru Tegh Bahadur had sacrificed his head, but not his religion, even they would sacrifice their heads, for their religion. In a pandal, about 50,000 Sikhs were seated. Just in front of that canopy, was a silk canopy.

Guru Govind Singh did the sacrificial prayer and then, went into the tent behind this canopy. After sometime, he returned, took his sword out and said, "I want a head. Is there anyone, who can sacrifice his head, in the name of the Guru?" There was pin-drop silence.

"I present my head, Oh Honourable one! The Real King!", said Lahore resident Dayaram, suddenly. "Then, come to me," said Guru Govind Singh. Fearlessly, the youth came and stood before Guru Govind Singh. Guruji took him inside the tent. After sometime, a sound was heard from inside. It felt as if Guruji had cut off Dayaram's head in one blow only. A stream of blood started flowing out from the tent. "I need one more head," he said. "Is there any brave person, who can give his head to the Goddess of Power? There was an even greater silence now. Then, Dharamdas, a resident of Delhi, came and stood with his head bent down, before Guruji. He was also taken inside the tent and the same thing was done. This happened three times more and three youths - Bhai Mohanchand of Dwarka and Bhai Sahebchand and Bhai Himmat Rai of Bidar, came and stood before him. People outside thought that these three had also been sacrificed at the altar of the Goddess.

When he came out of the tent, Guruji got a fire lit and placed a huge pan on top of it. He got it filled with water and while reciting the words of the Gurus; he stared stirring the water with his big, broad sword. Mata Sundri put some "batashas" (semi-spherical, hard and crisp sugar cakes) into it. When the batashas melted in the water and the recitation was complete, Guruji removed the curtains from the tent. The eyes of the Sikhs sitting in the pandal, popped out in surprise. All the five youths dressed in brave attire were standing before them.

Guruji gave the nectar to all five of them, from the vessel and then, drank it himself from their hands. Then he made the proclamation, "From today, I change my name, from Govind Rai to Govind Singh. Similarly, from today, Singh will be added to the names of all Sikhs. Their children will also have Singh added to their names. From today, the Sikhs will consider themselves, as strong as lions."

"The Sikh panth will be known as the Khalsa panth. Khalsa means war. Those who follow this path will also be called Khalsa. From today, after having this nectar, no Sikh shall cut his hair. He will have to keep the five "Ks" with him, all the time. These are "Kaccha" (underpants), "Kesh" (hair), "Kada" (steel bangle), "Kataar" (dagger) and "Kanghaa" (comb). He shall have to vow that whenever his religion is in danger, he shall sacrifice his all. Like these five lions, he shall not fear death." The entire pandal reverberated with the sound of "Vahe Guruji ka Khalsa! Vahe Guruji ki Fateha!" (Long live guruji's Khalsa, victory be to Guruji). When the assembly was dismissed, one could hear sounds of "Jo bole so Nihal; Sat Sri Akaal"[*]

◻◻

And this roar of the lions, reached the hill kings, in the mountains around Anandpur. They lost their peace and their nights' sleep. They started shaking with fear of the rising military power of Govind Singh. They used to all pay annual tax to the Mughal emperor. They had accepted their supremacy. But Delhi was still far. They had no hope of Aurangzeb's help and if he did send his army, it would take them so long to reach there, that the Sikh army would destroy them completely by then. They decided to attack Anandpur simultaneously. But Guru Govind Singh's "Veer Vahini" (brave riders) stopped the hill kings at a place called Bhangani and attacked them like hawks. This was the first test of the bravery and valour of Guru Govind Singh and his Khalsa army. The combined army of the hill kings could not face the army of the lions and ran away, leaving all their arms and ammunitions behind. War had been necessary. Therefore, Guru Govind Singh got Lohgarh and five other solid forts built and filled them with arms and ammunitions.

◻◻

Aurangzeb's spies were giving all the information about every step of Guru Govind Singh. His growing strength angered Aurangzeb. When he heard that Guru Govind Singh had given a crushing defeat to the hill kings twice, and had now started charging them "chauth" (one fourth), he started spitting fire.

He ordered Wazir Khan, the subehdar of Punjab, to destroy the power of the Sikhs, arrest Guru Govind Singh and present him in the courts of Delhi. Wazir Khan left with a huge army for Anandpur. Guru Govind Singh came to know about the activities of the Mughal army. He closed the main entrance to the fort and started preparing to face the Mughal army. Wazir Khan's massive army surrounded the fort from all sides. Wazir Khan ordered the army to break the door of the fort and enter, but the Sikhs showered so many arrows from within the fort, that the men could not come near the door.

In the darkness of the night, the Sikhs would come out of the fort and attack the sleeping Mughal army and after killing thousands of soldiers, would return inside the fort. And the door would be shut again. The Mughal army started reducing, but Wazir Khan did not withdraw his forces. He stayed there for six months, surrounding Anandpur.

The Anandpur fort ran short of provisions. Yet, Guru Govind Singh did not lose heart. One day, he came out with his Sikh warriors and attacked the Mughal forces so suddenly, that the Mughal army did not get a chance to pick up arms. They all ran away. They Sikh army not only became victorious, it also got a lot of arms and ammunition.

Defeated, Wazir Khan returned to Lahore. When Aurangzeb heard this, he was furious. He sent an even bigger force to attack Anandpur. The Mughal army surrounded Anandpur like locusts, but the Commander had realised that he would not be able to defeat the Sikh army by surrounding the fort for six months. So, they planned to use deceit. They sent a message to Guru Govind Singh that they only want the fort of Anandpur. If he laves the fort and goes away, the Mughal army will end the war. Later on, even the fort would be returned to them.

Guru Govind Sigh sent the women and children to safe places, but the moment he came out of the fort with the army, the Mughal army surrounded them. A massive battle took place. The Sikh warriors also fought bravely, but they were not prepared for this sudden attack. Guru Govind Singh had not even dreamt that he would be cheated this way. Each Sikh warrior killed ten Mughal warriors, before dying and reached Chamkor.

□□

Guru Govind Singh first got married in 1734 to a girl called Jito. He had three sons - Jujhar Singh, Joravar Singh and Fateh Singh. Te second wife's name was Sundari, who gave birth to Ajit Singh. The third time he got married to Deva. She had no children. Guru Govind Singh told her to consider the Khalsa panth as her child. That is why, even today, the Sikhs consider Guru Govind Singh as their religious father and Mata Deva as their mother.

When Guru Govind Singh left Anandpur, he got all his treasures filled in gunny bags and got them placed in a boat. His two sons, Joravar Singh and Fateh Singh and his mother, Gujri, were also in that boat. He told his trusted cook, Gangu Brahmin, to take them to his house for a few days, as they will be out of sight of the Mughal soldiers.

But, when he saw so much wealth, Gangu became greedy. So, he informed the Mughal ruler, that Guru Govind Singh's sons and mother were hiding in his house. He was awarded for being a traitor and Guru Govind Singh's mother and two sons, were presented before subehdar Wazir Khan of Punjab. Seeing their glowing faces, Wazir Khan thought he would convert them to Islam. This would not only benefit Islam, it would also lower the morale of the Sikhs. He told the children, "Your father has been defeated in war. So, he has run away. You accept Islam. We'll keep you with love and respect. You will also receive a lot of property." But, both the brave children had the blood of Guru Tegh Bahadur and warrior Guru Govind Singh. Fearlessly, they answered, "We cannot leave our religion. No amount of temptation can make us stray from the path of religion." Wazir Khan told them that they would be killed if they did not listen to him. But, they did not agree. So, the subehdar ordered that they be cemented into the wall. They were both made to stand together and a wall started being built around them. Both the boys closed their eyes and started chanting prayers. Soon, the wall covered them up. When their grandmother heard of their death, she jumped down from the tower and killed herself.

At that time, Guru Govind Singh was in the Chamkor Fort. The Mughal army had surrounded it from all four sides. His two sons, Ajit Singh and Jujhar Singh, were both killed, while leading the army. When he got the news of the death of his two other sons, Guru Govind Singh was not perturbed at all. Very fearlessly, he said, "So what if I have sacrificed four of my sons, for safeguarding my country and religion? I still have thousands of sons left."

It was necessary to organise a new army to fight the war of Chamkor. So, he started going to different places, to encourage Sikhs to join the army. He was camping in one place, when the Mughal soldiers surrounded them. Suddenly, a Sikh soldier picked up two swords in both hands, dressed up like Guru Govind Singh and started fighting the Mughal army. Thinking that he was Guru Govind Singh, the Mughals stared chasing him. Guru Govind Singh took this opportunity to escape from there. Similarly, once, when near a village, the Mughal army surrounded him, two Pathans made him sit in a palenquin and it started for another village.

The Mughal soldiers asked, "Who is in the palenquin?" the two Pathans answered, "Our Pir (saint). Don't you dare touch it." The Mughals were well aware of the determination and bravery of the Pathans. They gave them permission to go. The two pathans moved the palenquin towards the dense forest.

When the man, who had been dressed as Guru Govind Singh, died, Wazir Khan thought that Guru Govind Singh had been killed. So, he retuned with his forces to Lahore.
Guru Govind Singh was planning to go to the South. When Aurangzeb suddenly died and his sons started fighting amongst themselves for the throne. His son, Muazzam, had met Guru Govind Singh earlier also. He was his admirer. He had even pleaded for help. Guru Govind Singh had a small army at that time. Yet, he helped Prince Muazzam. He won and ruled over Delhi as Bahadur Shah. He was not a fanatic like his father. Besides, he knew that the Mughal army had lost its power. Shivaji in the South and Chhatrasal, the ruler of Oreha in Bundelkhand,

had shaken the roots of the Mughal Empire. Bahadur Shah invited guru Govind Singh to Delhi. He was welcomed and a promise was given that the Mughals would not bother the Sikhs anymore.

Guru Govind Singh stayed in Delhi for a few days and then, reached the banks of the river Godavari, where he saw a massive monastery. A recluse named Madhodas used to live here. When Guruji asked him his name, he said he was his disciple and came to be known as 'Banda Vairagi'.

Banda Vairagi had got the news of Punjab from the pilgrims and heard of the Muslim atrocities on the Hindus. When he heard of the killing of Guru Govind Singh's sons, his anger erupted like a volcano. He vowed that he would kill those who had cemented Guru Govind Singh's sons in the wall. He took permission from Guruji, gave the monastery to him, took all his property and a few Sikhs and went to Punjab.

After Aurangzeb's death, the atmosphere in Punjab had become peaceful. Banda Vairagi organised a massive force of the Sikhs and the Hindus and fell on the Mughals like lightening. They brought down the fort. Practically, all the Mughals were killed. Those that were left, ran away.

Banda Vairagi arrested the ruler and very cruelly, killed him. After taking control of Sarhind, Banda Vairagi's forces marched towards Lahore. He wanted to kill Wazir Khan, the subehdar, in a similar manner because he had given the order to cement Guruji's children into the wall.

The Sikh army encircled the Lahore fort. War with the Mughal army went on for a number of days. In the end, the Mughals ran away. Banda Vairagi killed Wazir Khan mercilessly. After avenging the death of Guruji's sons also, the fire of revenge did not subside. So, he organised the army and fought to get back all Guru Govind Singh's forts, now under Mughal control, and the Mughal forts too. The Mughal soldiers started leaving Punjab at the mere mention of Banda Vairagi's name, who had occupied the entire Punjab- from haryana to the border province.

One night, Guruji was sleeping in his camp. Suddenly, two Pathans, taking advantage of the darkness, infiltrated into the camp. When he heard the sound, Guruji awoke, quickly picked up his sword and roasted the Pathan's head. But, in the meantime, the other Pathan stabbed him in the back and ran away. By then, the

Sikhs who had come with Guruji awoke. They ran after the fleeing Pathan and cut him into pieces.

The wound on Guru Govind Singh's back was very deep, but it healed slowly. He had not recovered properly yet when, while threading the bow, the wound opened up again. A lot of treatment was done, but the wound became worse.

Guru Govind Singh was only 41 years old but seeing his ill health, he guessed that his end time had come. He called his Sikh friends and said, "My end has come near. I may not be able to see the morning Sun. After me; the Sikhs will not have any guru. After me, you consider Guru Granth Saheb as your guru and receive orders from it. Guru Granth Saheb only will guide you."

After giving the last order to the Sikhs, he abandoned his body and died.

That was the dark night of the 7th of October 1708.

❏ ❏ ❏

Diamond Pocket Books

Presents in OSHO BOOKS
Osho's illuminating and enlightening discourse

Title	Price
I am the Gate	150.00
The Great Challenge	150.00
Meditation: The Art of Ecstasy	150.00
I Say unto You-I& II (Each)	150.00
Zen and the Art of Living	150.00
Zen and the Art of Enlightenment	150.00
Zen: Take it Easy	150.00
Zen: And the Art of Meditation	15.00
The Psychology of the Escoteric	150.00
The Divine Melody	100.00
A Cup of Tea	150.00
And the flowers Showered	100.00
The Mystery Beyond Mind	50.00
The Forgotten Language of the Heart	35.00
The Alpha and The Omega	
Cessation of the Mind	50.00
The Birth of Being	50.00
From Choas to Cosmos	60.00
The Ever Present Flower	60.00
Towards the Unknown	40.00
Bauls : The Dancing Mastics	35.00
Bauls: The Seekers of the Path	35.00
Bauls: The Mystics of Celebration	35.00
Bauls: The Singing Mystics	35.00
Ecstasy : The Language Of Existence	50.00
Be Oceanic	50.00
The Greatest Gamble	40.00
Vedante : The Ultimate Truth	40.00
Vedanta: The First Star in The Evening	40.00
Vedanta: An Art of Dying	40.00
A Taste of the Divine	50.00
One Earth One Humanity	50.00
Love and Meditation	40.00
Freedom from the Mind	40.00
Life, A Song, A Dance	40.00
Meeting the Ultimate	40.00
The Master is a Mirror	40.00
The Alchemy of Enlightenment	40.00
From Lgnorance to Innocence	40.00
Be Silent and Know	40.00
Tantra Vision: The Secret of the Inner Experience	40.00
Tantra Vision: The Door to Nirvana	40.00
Tantra Vision :Beyond The Barriers of Wisdom	40.00
Eternal Celebration	40.00
A Song without Words	40.00
Inner Harmony	40.00
Sing, Dance, Rejoice	40.00
Secret of Disciplehood	40.00
Laughter is My Message	40.00
The Centre of the Cyclone Meditation : The Ultimate Adventure	40.00
Sufi Peaple of the Path	
A Lotus of Emptiness	150.00
The Royal Way	150.00
Glory of Freedom	150.00
Singing Silence	150.00
The Alpha and the Omega (Part 3-10)(In Press)	

Diamond Pocket Books Pvt.Ltd.
X-30, Okhla Industrial Area,
Phase- II, New Delhi-110020
Phone : 011-6841033, 6822803-4, Fax : 91-11-6925020

DIAMOND POCKET BOOKS PRESENTS

Dictionaries   Price
Diamond English-English-Hindi Dictionary 180.00
Diamond English-Hindi Dictionary 150.00
Diamond Hindi-English Dictionary 150.00
Diamond English-Hindi Dictionary 60.00
Diamond Hindi-English Dictionary 60.00
Diamond Hindi Dictionary 100.00
Diamond Hindi Dictionary 75.00
Diamond Hindi Dictionary 50.00
Diamond Dictionary (Student Edition) 40.00
Diamond Hindi-English Dictionary (Student Edition) 40.00
Diamond English-Hindi Dictionary (Student Edition) 40.00
Diamond Anglo-Assamese Pocket Dictionary (2 coloured) 60.00
Diamond Anglo-Assamese Pocket Dictionary 30.00

Language Series
Diamond English Speaking Course (Hindi) 70.00
Diamond English Speaking Course (Bengali) 70.00
Diamond English Speaking Course (Assamese) 70.00
Diamond English Speaking Course (Nepali) 70.00
Diamond English Speaking Course (Gujarati) 50.00
Diamond English Speaking Course (Marathi) 50.00
Learn and Speak 15 Indian Languages (by P. Machwe) 40.00
Learn English in 30 Days 30.00
Learn English through Bengali 20.00
Learn Nepali through English 20.00

DIAMOND POCKET BOOKS
X-30, Okhla Industrial Area, Phase-II,
New Delhi-110020
Ph. No.6841033, 6822803-4, Fax : 91- 011- 6925020
E-mail : mverma@nde.vsnl.net.in
Website : www.diamondpocketbooks.com